# SIX
# IMAGES OF
# HUMAN NATURE

# SIX
# IMAGES OF
# HUMAN NATURE

Norman Chaney

Prentice Hall
Englewood Cliffs, New Jersey 07632

Library of Congress Cataloging-in-Publication Data

Chaney, Norman.
  Six images of human nature/Norman Chaney.
    p.  cm.
  Includes bibliographical references.
  ISBN 0-13-812033-1
  1. Man.  2. Philosophical anthropology.  I. Title.  II. Title: 6
images of human nature.
BD450.C472  1990
128—dc20                                    89-39250
                                               CIP

*Editorial/production supervision and*
    *interior design:* Laura L. Cleveland
*Cover design:* Wanda Lubelska
*Manufacturing buyer:* Carol Bystrom

1990 by Prentice-Hall, Inc.
A Division of Simon & Schuster
Englewood Cliffs, New Jersey 07632

Printed in the United States of America
10  9  8  7  6  5  4  3  2  1


ISBN 0-13-812033-1


Prentice-Hall International (UK) Limited, *London*
Prentice-Hall of Australia Pty. Limited, *Sydney*
Prentice-Hall Canada Inc., *Toronto*
Prentice-Hall Hispanoamericana, S.A., *Mexico*
Prentice-Hall of India Private Limited, *New Delhi*
Prentice-Hall of Japan, Inc., *Tokyo*
Simon & Schuster Asia Pte. Ltd., *Singapore*
Editora Prentice-Hall do Brasil, Ltda., *Rio de Janeiro*

*To Elizabeth and Paul*

# CONTENTS

**Preface**    xi

**Acknowledgments**    xiii

**Introduction**    1

Approaching Human Nature    3
Darwin's Partial Image of Human Nature    8
Formulating Our Own Image of Human Nature    13
Looking Toward the Following Chapters    16
*Suggestions for Discussion and Study*    18
*Further Reading*    19
*Notes*    19

**1 Confucius and the Image of the Individual in Society    21**

Cultural Background    23
Biography    24
Confucius on What Can I Know?    26
Confucius on What Ought I to Do?    28
Confucius on for What Can I Hope?    34
Implications of the Confucian Image of Human Nature    36
*Suggestions for Discussion and Study*    38

*Further Reading*    39
*Notes*    40

## 2 Sophocles and the Image of Tragic Heroism    43

Cultural Background    45
Biography    48
Sophocles and the Legend of Oedipus    48
Sophocles on What Can I Know?    54
Sophocles on What Ought I to Do?    56
Sophocles on for What Can I Hope?    58
Implications of the Sophoclean Image of
    Human Nature    61
*Suggestions for Discussion and Study*    62
*Further Reading*    64
*Notes*    65

## 3 Augustine and the Image of Faith    67

Cultural Background    69
Biography    70
Augustine on What Can I Know?    74
Augustine on What Ought I to Do?    78
Augustine on for What Can I Hope?    82
Implications of the Augustinian Image of
    Human Nature    86
*Suggestions for Discussion and Study*    89
*Further Reading*    90
*Notes*    90

## 4 Thomas Hobbes and the Image of Egoism    93

Cultural Background    95
Biography    97
Hobbes on What Can I Know?    101
Hobbes on What Ought I to Do?    105
Hobbes on for What Can I Hope?    110

Implications of the Hobbesian Image of
Human Nature    111
*Suggestions for Discussion and Study*    112
*Further Reading*    114
*Notes*    115

## 5  David Hume and the Image of Sympathy    117

Cultural Background    119
Biography    120
Hume on What Can I Know?    124
Hume on What Ought I to Do?    128
Hume on for What Can I Hope?    132
Implications of the Humian Image of Human Nature    134
*Suggestions for Discussion and Study*    136
*Further Reading*    138
*Notes*    139

## 6  John Dewey and the Image of Change    141

Cultural Background    143
Biography    144
Dewey on What Can I Know?    147
Dewey on What Ought I to Do?    151
Dewey on for What Can I Hope?    154
Implications of the Deweyan Image of Human Nature
156
*Suggestions for Discussion and Study*    159
*Further Reading*    161
*Notes*    161

## Conclusion    163

*Note*    168

## Index    169

# Preface

This book explores six thinkers' views of human nature. At the center of every serious view of human nature stand three questions: What can I know? What ought I to do? For what can I hope? How a thinker answers these questions constitutes his or her view of human nature. Our task as readers is to bring these answers out of the background of a thinker's work, where they often lie, and see what comes of holding them up to the light.

The main theoretical features of the book are set forth in the Introduction. Each succeeding chapter brings these features to bear on the study of a particular thinker. If the book is pursued sequentially, chapter by chapter, the reader gets a sense of how views of human nature have unfolded over a period of twenty-five hundred years. But, since no single thread of argument—no particular view of human nature I am seeking to defend or develop—runs through the book, it's not essential to read it sequentially. Occasionally, I compare one thinker to another, but this technique is not extensive and should not handicap studying the thinkers independently. Each chapter is essentially self-contained.

My dominant task has been to present some major views of human nature that have existed in the past and exist in the present. Studying other thinkers' answers to the questions of human nature does not take the place of formulating our own, but it can help us clarify our own. I offer this book in the spirit of urging readers to answer the deeply personal questions of human nature for themselves.

My thanks to Professors Hugh Burtner and James R. Bailey for their encouragement in the writing of this book, and to my wife, Hilde.

# Acknowledgments

Quotations from *The Analects of Confucius*, translated and annotated by Arthur Waley (New York: Random House, Vintage Books, 1938) reprinted with permission of Macmillan Publishing Company. Copyright 1939 by George Allen and Unwin, Ltd.; copyright renewed © 1966 by Unwin Hyman Limited.

Quotations from *Oedipus the King* (trans. David Grene), *Oedipus at Colonus* (trans. Robert Fitzgerald), and *Antigone* (trans. Elizabeth Wyckoff) reprinted with permission from *Sophocles I* in *The Complete Greek Tragedies*, trans. Grene and Lattimore (Chicago: University of Chicago Press, 1954). © 1954 by The University of Chicago. All rights reserved.

Quotations from Jo Ann Boydston, ed., *How We Think: A Restatement of the Relation of Reflective Thinking to the Educative Process* by John Dewey, Vol. 8 of *John Dewey: The Later Works, 1925–1953* (Carbondale: Southern Illinois University Press, 1986), pp. 121–122, reprinted with permission from Southern Illinois University Press.

Quotations from Jo Ann Boydston, ed., *Does Human Nature Change?* by John Dewey, Vol. 13 of *John Dewey: The Later Works, 1925–1953* (Carbondale: Southern Illinois University Press, 1988), p. 286, reprinted with permission from Southern Illinois University Press.

Quotations from Jo Ann Boydston, ed., *Ethics* by John Dewey, Vol. 7 of *John Dewey: The Later Works, 1925–1953* (Carbondale: Southern Illinois University Press, 1985), p. 184, reprinted with permission from Southern Illinois University Press.

All our endeavours or desires so follow from the necessity of our nature, that they can be understood either through it alone, as their proximate cause, or by virtue of our being a part of nature, which cannot be adequately conceived through itself without other individuals.

—Benedict Spinoza
*The Ethics*, Part IV, Appendix

# INTRODUCTION

# Approaching Human Nature

Human nature is a perplexing subject, and we'd best indicate from the outset what we're talking about when we address it. For many thousands of years, the human being, *Homo sapiens*, has had the ability to recognize himself or herself as somehow standing apart from, yet being related to, all other creatures. The notion that differences, not merely in degree but in kind, exist between humans and other creatures has been handed down from the time of Greek antiquity under the rubric human nature. Definitions of what constitutes this nature, however, have varied widely. Where one thinker might speak of the human being as the "reasoning" animal, others might speak of the "tool-making" or the "language-using" or the "worshipping" animal. Herein lies a basic perplexity of the subject. In entertaining various definitions of human nature, we begin to find ourselves more confused than enlightened.

We can impose some order on our understanding of the subject if we speak of three kinds of human nature, each of which inspires a differing mode of study. The first kind is *original* human nature: human life as it has developed through evolutionary processes. It explains how human life-forms differ organically from those of other creatures. The second is *cultural* human nature. It explains how humans, as distinguished from other creatures, have shaped and remade the world in accordance with their social needs. The third is *autonomous* human nature: human nature as it is manifested in the life of the person. It explains how individuals, in unique, self-chosen ways, express their difference not only from other creatures but also from other persons.[1]

Anybody who studies human nature is limited by his or her own predispositions. Omniscience is not a human attribute: as individuals we are limited by what we desire to know, do know, and can know. Thus, it's impossible for any individual to deliver the final word on human nature. But it is possible to be aware of our modes of study and to speak meaningfully within them. In this book we'll touch on original human nature (in discussing Darwin), but we're primarily concerned with cultural and autonomous human nature, which find their correlative modes of study within the disciplines of the humanities. Part of the legitimacy of this approach is the need to bring the idea of human nature to the forefront in modern humanistic studies.

In his *Reflections on Human Nature*, A. O. Lovejoy writes:

> The history of the theory of human nature—of men's ideas about man— . . . is, or should be, one of the major fields of investigation for the student of the history of ideas. . . . We have many works, under various titles, on the history of the idea of God, but none that I can recall on the history of the idea of man.[2]

Lovejoy is convinced that great periods of intellectual achievement may be distinguished from one another by referring to the characterizations, or images, of human nature they fashion. Moreover, he perceives that these images, latent and unexamined though they may be, "are important phenomena in the history of the human mind."[3] Such images have the power to shape the thought and conduct not merely of individuals but of whole peoples. They present a picture, or idea, of what the human being is and what the potentials of humankind are. They are models to live by.

Another thinker who speaks of the power of images is the philosopher Karl Jaspers. He writes:

> Men cannot live without images of themselves. . . . Images have surrounded man at all times: in mythological figures of heroes, in Greek gods, who were consubstantial with man but differed from him only in being immortal. Images surround him in the figures of sages, prophets, saints, in figures of poetry. How do they surround him today? Are there still guiding images that appear to us?[4]

Both Lovejoy and Jaspers are pointing to the significant role images play in helping us define ourselves, in giving us a sense of what it means to be human. Every image of human nature contains an *ought*, even if its content is only that humanity should be what the facts appear to report. And every *ought* about humanity eventually attempts to rest its interpretation on an *is*, even if the real *is* is regarded as being far removed from its appearance. Is there anybody who does not dwell—in agreement or in conflict, in compliance or repudiation, with good or bad conscience—in some image of his or her own nature? As we begin to think about images of human nature, we soon realize we are actually thinking about our own lives.

No source of images is more insistent than the early training a child receives from his or her elders (parents, grandparents). When, for example, an elder encourages a child to be resolute, truthful, and cooperative, as opposed to irresolute, untruthful, and uncooperative, some notion of *ideal* conduct is operative. Where do such notions reside if not in prior images of human nature, those pictures that are carried in the mind and transmitted from one generation to another?

In the course of maturing, however, individuals increasingly reach outside their immediate nurturing circle, discovering that various images of human nature, especially as embodied in films, literature, philosophy, psychology, religion, and science, compete for their attention. More often than not, this competition produces a sense of conflict in the individual. The only way to deal with this conflict is to confront it: we sort out various images of human nature—tugging this way and that—and weigh them one against the other as the means of arriving at one we can claim as our own.

When we speak in terms of *images*, we aren't raising the deeply philosophical question of what human nature is as a *thing-in-itself*. With the concept of images we are moving away from questions of pure being toward questions about ourselves as thinking creatures. Instead of trying to say what the human *really is*, we are concerned with trying to say what the human *thinks* he or she is.

The philosopher Hans Vaihinger (1852–1933) has exactingly worked out a theory of knowledge, rooted in the writings of Immanuel Kant (1724–1804), in his book *The Philosophy of 'As If.'* Vaihinger expresses the essence of this theory in the following words:

> However we may conceive the relation of thought and reality, it may be asserted from the empirical point of view, that the ways of thought are different from those of reality, the subjective processes of thought concerned with any given external event or process have very rarely a demonstrable similarity to it.[5]

Here and throughout his book, Vaihinger is expressing a *hypothetical* theory of knowledge, according to which the whole

5

world of thought is an instrument that enables us to orient ourselves in the real world, but thoughts are not a copy of the real world. Ideas, in other words, are artifices of the real world, which are strikingly purposive expressions of the function of thought.[6] In light of this theory, it's possible to explain more deliberately what we mean in the context of this book when we speak in terms of images. Images are *ideas* of human nature: they are instruments of thought that enable us to orient ourselves to life.

Images play a profound role in major living religions, where they have crystallized around luminous, exemplary historical figures. Within Christianity, for instance, the notion that human beings are created in the image of God is a basic tenet of belief. What does it mean, we might ask, to be created in the image of God? Christians respond by pointing to the historical figure of Jesus as the manifestation of the divine image. Not a day passes in the Christian world without the image of Jesus being held up—in sermon, hymn, and other forms of worship—as the model of imitation. Literally millions of people throughout the world attempt to conduct their lives in conformity with the life of Jesus. He prevails upon the mind of Christians—as does Mahomet upon the mind of Muslims or Moses upon the mind of Jews or Siddhartha Gautama upon the mind of Buddhists—as an image of how the human being ought to conduct his or her life.

As models for the conduct of life, images of human nature touch us at a deeply personal level. Nobody can decide *for* us what images ought to guide our lives. Sören Kierkegaard (1813–1855) was well aware of the importance of discovering our own images when he wrote, "The thing is to find a truth which is true *for me, to find the idea for which I can live and die.*"[7] Kierkegaard did not mean, however, that just any truth would suffice when it comes to so fundamental a matter as committing ourselves to an idea that is synonymous with life itself. The precise object of the commitment is all-important. Images of human nature abound that are merely *partial*, that do not yield a *complete* picture of life. Later, we will say more about partial images in discussing the thought of Charles Darwin. For now, let's talk about complete images, the kind that command the deepest of personal loyalties.

No thinker was better equipped intellectually than Kant to help us understand the character of a complete image of human nature. In his lectures on logic, Kant pointed out that the idea of human nature subsumes three basic, perennial questions of existence: *What can I know? What ought I to do? For what can I hope?* Within the discipline of philosophy, these questions belong to the areas of epistemology, morality, and religion, respectively.

But Kant insisted these three questions come together within philosophy in the area of anthropology, which tries to answer them summarily. According to him, anthropology strives to completely interpret human nature; it tries to comprehend the boundaries of being human.[8] In this book, when we speak of a complete image of human nature, we have in mind the kind of thought Kant associated with anthropology. A complete image of human nature is a synthetic, interpretive picture of human life, which a thinker formulates in the course of working out his or her own responses to the basic questions of existence.

Thus far in our discussion, we have (1) indicated that images have a great power to influence our lives; (2) presented the notion that an image of human nature is an instrument of thought that enables us to orient ourselves to life; and (3) explained what we mean by a complete image of human nature. Let's keep these principles in mind as we reflect further on images of human nature and pursue reasons for studying them.

There is seemingly no more important single element in the dynamics of culture than a complete image of human nature. It operates as both cause and effect: as effect, inasmuch as it starts from and is limited by an interpretation of human life that is current at the time of its origin; as cause, inasmuch as, in the further course of time, the image itself helps bring about the formation and fixation of habits of thought and conduct divergent from those that prevailed before it. From these diverging habits of thought and conduct, from this differing interpretation of human life as their base, subsequent thinkers will start to formulate a new image of human nature.

In every culture at least one thinker is regarded as representative of the culture itself, such as each of the six main thinkers presented in this book. Confucius represents the culture of ancient China; Sophocles, ancient Greece; Augustine, the late Roman Empire and Middle Ages; Thomas Hobbes, the late Renaissance; David Hume, the Enlightenment; and John Dewey, our own period. These thinkers have defined what it's meant to be human in their own time and place. In studying the images they have formulated, we gain some sense of Lovejoy's history of the idea of human nature over a span of twenty-five hundred years.

7

The governing question in the study of the history of images, however, is finally a personal one. What is *my* image of human nature? Who am I in relation to images of the past? It's neither possible nor even desirable to break completely with images of the past. But it is possible and appropriate to vitalize them, to shape them anew, and to reply to the opposition they offer with the formulation of our own images. By becoming more cognizant and critical of images of the past, we realize possibilities that can lead us into the future.

If we undertake this task of formulating our own image of human nature based on the study of others', we should keep in mind that not all images are complete in the sense we have previously outlined. Some are only partial, responding perhaps to only one or two of Kant's three basic questions of existence. This partiality of an image, however, does not necessarily diminish its power to influence our lives. Indeed, one of the most influential images in our time—that which emerges in the thought of Charles Darwin—is a partial one. (In Chapter 6, we'll have more to say about how the Darwinian image is assimilated in the thought of John Dewey.)

## Darwin's Partial Image of Human Nature

Darwin (1809–1882) was born into an English family distinguished for its scientific, philosophical, and artistic achievements. After his formal education, he accepted the unpaid position of naturalist aboard the H. M. S. *Beagle*, which was to make a scientific expedition for several years to the South Seas. This voyage marked a turning point in Darwin's life, for it led him directly to the geological and biological speculations that were to blossom into his theory of biological evolution through natural selection. Briefly expressed, this theory posits that the whole world of living things is related, having developed from the very simplest forms of life. The human being belongs to the highest class, namely, the mammals of the great group of vertebrate animals. Among mammals the human being is a primate who stands at the top of this order, which includes apes, monkeys, and lemurs.

Although Darwin's name has become synonymous with the theory of biological evolution, he by no means invented the idea. Aristotle, not Darwin, wrote: "Nature proceeds little by little from things lifeless to animal life in such a way that it is impossible to determine the exact line of demarcation, nor on which side thereof an intermediate form should lie."[9] Philosophers and scientists had thus been speculating about the evolution of life for more than two thousand years. During the nineteenth century, ideas of biological evolution were part of the intellectual climate, waiting to be expressed in some unifying theory. Only eleven months before the publication of *On the Origin of the Species* in 1859, Darwin discovered that fellow Englishman Alfred Russel Wallace (1823–1913) had reached a theory of evolution similar to his own.

The broad explanatory scheme of evolution as set forth by Darwin rests on four basic tenets: (1) The world is evolving. Species change continually; new ones originate and others become extinct. (2) Evolution is gradual, or continuous. It does not consist of discontinuous saltations (i.e., leaps or sudden changes). (3) Similar organisms are related, having descended from a common ancestor. In fact, all living organisms are related to a single origin of life. (4) Evolutionary change is the result of selection. It is this fourth tenet, natural selection—popularly described as survival of the fittest—that often symbolizes the whole of Darwin's theory of evolution.

For him, however, evolution and natural selection were not the same thing. The first is the transformation of the species over the course of many generations. The second is a two-step process that causes these changes to take place. Natural selection is Darwin's mechanism, or hypothesis, that explains evolutionary change.

The first step of natural selection is variation in a given species. In every generation, a great amount of variation is generated. Darwin did not know the source of this variation, but he recognized it on the basis of empirical observation, as in his study of finches in the Galapagos Islands.

The second step is selection through survival in the struggle for existence. In most species of animals and plants, a set of parents produces thousands of offspring. Very few of those offspring survive. The survivors have the most appropriate combinations of characters for coping with the environment, including climate, competitors, and enemies. The advantageous hereditary characters of survivors are passed on to subsequent generations, thus ensuring the evolution of the species.

Darwin's theory of evolution is strictly scientific in that it limits itself to what can, in principle, be confirmed or falsified by appropriate scientific methods. Evolution itself does not necessarily mean the movement of humanity to a desirable goal; it's a neutral scientific concept, compatible with either optimism or pessimism. According to different interpretations, it may appear to be a steady amelioration or a guarantee of destruction. Indeed, at differing moments in his career, Darwin himself interpreted it both ways. Speaking as an optimist, Darwin paints a picture of humanity's steady progress toward an ever brighter future.

> Man may be excused for feeling some pride at having risen, though not through his own exertions, to the very summit of the organic scale; and the fact of his having thus risen, instead of having been aboriginally placed there, may give him hope for a still higher destiny in the distant future.[10]

When the whole picture is unfolded, however, Darwin wasn't actually optimistic about the human prospect. His central vision is contained in a cryptic notation he committed to his notebooks where, speaking as a pessimist, he wrote: "If all men were dead, then monkeys make men.—Men make angels."[11] Considered in the larger context of Darwin's thought, this notation may be read on at least two levels. He is suggesting that in nature organisms evolve in such a manner that they fill up ecological niches. In this evolutionary process, there is a place for an intelligent, human-like creature. If the chancy mechanism of natural selection had not brought about *Homo sapiens*, a creature similar to us would have evolved because conditions favored it.[12] He is also suggesting that the continuation of the evolutionary process will bring forth something higher in the evolutionary scale than the human being—"angels." But for all of its glory, this idealized, angelic creature, too, will ultimately become extinct.

Darwin assumed that in the end, the sun and all the planets will grow too cold to support life. It was an idea, based on scientific evidence, over which he agonized.

> Believing as I do that man in the distant future will be a far more perfect creature than he now is, it is an intolerable

thought that he and all other sentient beings are doomed to complete annihilation after such long-continued slow progress.[13]

Although Darwin found the idea of human annihilation "intolerable," he nevertheless resigned himself to it.

Darwin was admittedly a thinker of scientific genius, but he did not go very far philosophically in formulating an image of human nature. In summing up his views, let's see to what extent he responds to the three basic questions of human existence. First, What can I know? is not answered by anything in Darwin's theory of evolution. He is hardly concerned with the knower's own individual experiences and personal reactions. He merely offers biological phenomena.

Second, he makes no attempt to answer the question What ought I to do? He merely intimates that *Homo sapiens*, in the process of evolution, has constantly achieved betterment.

Third, insofar as Darwin even approaches an answer to the question For what can I hope? the answer is a bleak one. From his perspective, *Homo sapiens* can neither do nor predict anything important about human destiny because the species is (1) necessarily a product of the evolutionary past; (2) necessarily moves forward to a future; and (3) that future, because of the principle of selection, is necessarily unpredictable. One cannot even say that the human creature has a *fate*, for in order to have one, there must be some ultimate Designer, Mind, or God who knows what that fate has in store.

The Darwinian theory of evolution is sometimes called the second Copernican revolution. Just as Copernicus showed that the earth is not the center of the solar system, so Darwin showed that the biological order does not revolve around the human being. The effect of Darwin's theory was to remove the human being from the center of the pattern of life and to place at that center the inexorable, all-consuming laws of evolution and natural selection.

Doubtless, the impact of Darwin's thought—his partial image of human nature—on our age has been enormous. This impact may be summarized in terms of our commonplace understanding of the transitoriness, mutability, and conflict inherent in all things human. Before Darwin, the idea of human nature implied a notion of sovereignty, humankind's privileged and purposeful status in the design of things. After Darwin, that idea of human sovereignty can no longer simply be taken for granted.

Is the Darwinian image of human nature an adequate model for living? For many, the question is already settled, because it's the model they tacitly accept. One suspects that literally millions of people, by virtue of having absorbed Darwinianism as if by osmosis, go to bed at night and wake in the morning with the vague perception that they are creatures caught up in a great evolutionary current that is sweeping them to some blind biological end. Franz Kafka's story "The Metamorphosis" renders the Darwinian image parabolically. The main character, Gregor Samsa, wakes one morning to find that he has been changed into a giant insect.

It's one thing to assume that Darwin's theory offers a plausible account of life on earth; it's quite another to assume that this is the whole account of humankind. From the point of view of this book, it's allowable to make the first assumption, but not the second. According to Darwin's image, all life is determined by outer circumstances and is dependent on acquired developments. It's a partial image that denies the freedom of human will in acts of choice.

If the idea of freedom is something we hold important, the Darwinian image can hardly be regarded as an adequate model for living. Vaihinger aptly points out that "there is nothing in the real world corresponding to the idea of [freedom]," but that "in practice it is an exceedingly necessary fiction."[14] It's necessary because, on the basis of this fiction or belief, we assume responsibility for our own lives.

What characterizes non-human creatures is their struggle to survive, to maintain their existence; what characterizes human beings is their ability and willingness to go beyond survival, to make choices, to be the pilot of their own destiny within the constraints—being born, growing old, and dying—imposed upon them by existence itself. Jean-Paul Sartre (1905–1980) has an odd but effective way of putting the matter: as humans, he says, we are "condemned to be free."[15]

Unless we wish to conceive of ourselves as a fortuitous combination of cells adrift on a vast sea of life, we must act as responsible persons. This means taking ourselves in hand, as it were, and making up our minds about the kinds of lives we want to live. The study of complete images of human nature can help us do just that, for they present us with the deepest challenges and with the broadest ways of thinking about the possibilities of human life.

## Formulating Our Own Image of Human Nature

An *assumption* is a proposition (i.e., an idea or a belief) that is accepted as plausible without clear proof to support it. We make assumptions in order to explore ideas that they can lead to. In this book, at least four main assumptions are operative in our whole approach to human nature. For the sake of clarity, a summary of them is in order.

The *first assumption* is that complete images of human nature conceptually bring human nature into view. No thinker formulates an image that exhausts all of the possibilities, however. Thought is culturally conditioned. To be sure, a thinker may formulate an image that is widely shared by persons of his or her own culture and even by persons of later cultures. But the possible ways of seeing what it means to be human are greater than any individual thinker can comprehend from his or her limited cultural perspective.

The *second assumption* is that we should be eclectic in our study of images, focusing on ideas, concepts, beliefs, and doctrines from a variety of models of human nature in the process of formulating our own. When images of human nature are regarded exclusively, they become irreconcilable conceptual blocks. From an eclectic point of view, however, a much more congenial situation emerges. Images of human nature, such as the six we are studying here, do not stand alone; the history of ideas suggests that they are contiguous.

The *third assumption* is that we have the capacity, if we only have the willingness, to move thoughtfully among images as a means of expanding our own horizons. The anthropologist Ruth Benedict has written:

> The truth of the matter is . . . that the possible human institutions and motives are legion, on every plane of cultural simplicity or complexity, and that wisdom consists in a greatly increased tolerance toward their divergencies.

No man can thoroughly participate in any culture unless he has been brought up and has lived according to its forms, but he can grant to other cultures the same significance to their participants which he recognizes in his own.[16]

Even though we each have *inherited* some image of human nature, partial or complete, we should apprise ourselves of others. Indeed, at our moment in history, the varieties of individual personality and the pluralities of culture provide an untold richness of opportunity for moving among many images of human nature.

The *fourth assumption* is the most basic in that it undergirds the other three. Earlier we spoke of the theory of knowledge which maintains that our ideas about the world are hypothetical in character. In light of this theory, no clear line separates appearance and reality, interpretation and fact. The world is as we see and interpret it, and the question of whether it is appropriate to see and interpret it in one way rather than another is to be decided on practical considerations: Does the holding of a particular image allow me to make sense of my own experience and to grasp what and who I am as a human being? Does it allow me to live in harmony with others? Does it satisfy my inmost needs and desires? Does it develop my life? We assume here that such questions can be answered only by individuals themselves.

It's one thing to maintain that there is knowledge from which all bias, conjecture, and question have been eliminated, but it's quite another to maintain that some of us have come to it fully. Images of human nature differ from one another because humans differ in the ways they see life. Dissent about the ways we see life is to be expected and even appreciated. Human beings need dissent, not for the sake of dissent or because it's absolute, but because it belongs to the process of learning. The human mind is an arguing activity. Through this activity opinions are shared, checks and balances are applied, understandings are formed, modified, broadened, and at times even harmonized with one another.

When we try to think openly about the meaning of images for ourselves, we're going to find, because of our prior convictions (unconscious or conscious, implicit or explicit), that we both agree and disagree with what others say and have said on the subject of human nature.

Let's suppose, by way of anticipating some of the thinkers we'll contend with in this book, that we're strongly attracted to the Sophoclean image of tragic heroism, and we believe with a modern thinker such as Albert Camus that tragic heroism is requisite for living. But at the same time, we're attracted to the Augustinian image of Christian humility, and we believe with a modern thinker such as Reinhold Niebuhr that tragic heroism is a pathetic form of human pride that denies the mercy of God.

In effect, neither the Sophoclean nor the Augustinian image is totally satisfying to us, since we *disagree* with both of them. Or, the problem may be expressed conversely. Neither image is totally satisfying to us because we *agree* with both of them. While both views have some claim on the image of human nature we are trying to arrive at for ourselves, neither has an exclusive claim on it.

The kind of conflict we would experience in this imagined situation could be nonetheless an occasion for personal insight and growth. We can and do agree and disagree with various thinkers' images of human nature, indicating that we have a power of discernment in relation to images. Such power marks the freedom we possess by virtue of being human.

It's impossible to specify the exact route a person should follow in arriving at his or her own image of human nature. But insofar as this book is to aid that task, let's suggest a way in which its presentation of models might be conceived.

Suppose it were possible for all of the thinkers we're studying here to gather for a kind of Socratic symposium in a large hall at a great university where hundreds of persons, including ourselves, are in attendance. The thinkers have been invited to engage in give-and-take conversation on the subject of human nature.

After we've listened to this conversation for a number of hours, one of the thinkers invites us to go home and write down what we understand to be our image of human nature. In composing our thoughts, we meditate on that conversation, bringing our own convictions, hidden in the deepest recesses of consciousness, to bear on the subject. When we aren't actually engaged in writing, we read whatever seems relevant to our subject and converse with others. We weigh various viewpoints, deciding whether to accept or reject them, and trying to give reasons for accepting or rejecting them. If we have been true to our task, we are then able to say, "This is my image of human nature, my pattern for the conduct of life."

It may not be the only image of human nature we'll ever profess. We are what we see, and as visual images change, so do we. But at least we can never be accused of having lived our lives unreflectively, never having asked in some significant depth what it means to be human. In effect, the presentation of thinkers in the six succeeding chapters is intended to initiate a conversation that will carry beyond the particular thinkers themselves.

## Looking toward the Following Chapters

Three main factors have played a part in selecting the thinkers whose images of human nature are presented here: (1) each represents a different culture; (2) each represents a serious option in our thinking about human nature today; and (3) each has had some particular appeal for the author of this book (the personal factor that emerges in any discussion of human nature).

Our basic scheme for studying each of these six main thinkers is as follows: First, we look at the thinker's cultural background and biography; second, we look at how he responds to each of the three Kantian questions of existence; third, we define the image of human nature that is indicated by his responses; and fourth, we consider how the thinker's image of human nature has influenced and continues to influence thought and conduct in the contemporary world. At the end of each chapter appear questions and observations to provoke further reflection, to serve as bases for discussion, and to afford insights for writing essays.

The following thumbnail sketches of each of the six main thinkers give an immediate sense of what lies ahead.

We start with Confucius and try to get beyond the naive notion that he was merely an orator of wise, pithy sayings. That notion comes to us, in part, because of the very form in which Confucius' teachings have been preserved, namely, in fragments that were recorded and shaped by his followers after his death. Confucius sees the human being as preeminently a social creature. In China's distant past, Confucius maintains, human beings lived well because they followed social traditions that had been divinely inspired (a strong theme of traditionalism runs throughout his teachings).

When we turn to Sophocles, we meet a thinker who was roughly contemporary with Confucius, but whose image of human nature differs markedly. Sophocles is not so much concerned with the possible harmony that can exist between human beings and the gods as with the disharmony that does exist. His dramatic symbol of human nature is Oedipus, the man who is punished by the gods for a sin his father committed before Oedipus was born. Undeserving of the fate that is visited upon him, he manages in spite of great suffering to hold his head high and assert his rightful place in the universe.

Augustine comes next. His is the only avowedly religious image of human nature we're studying. Whereas there are many interpretations of Christianity, Augustine's is located near the center of Christian orthodoxy. He projects an image of the human being as a creature who lives by faith, which has a profound effect on what a human being comes to know. A difficult concept, it's one that we'll consider carefully. It serves to counter any notion that faith is identical to intellectual poverty.

The ancient world ends in the West with Augustine. With Thomas Hobbes, we enter the Renaissance, that period generally recognized as the beginning of the modern world. Hobbes, who was much influenced by the scientific knowledge of his age, conceived of the universe as a vast mechanical order, which humans can come to understand thoroughly through the exercise of reason. The social order, however, is anything but orderly. The human being is fundamentally a ferocious animal, one who engages in war and pillage, always seeking his or her own gain. To insure a measure of peace within society, humans contract with each other to give up certain rights in order to obtain others. A strong ruler is required to guarantee these contracts are maintained.

After Hobbes we come to the Enlightenment and David Hume, who reverses Hobbes' views on reason and the ferocious nature of humans. He denies that reason can tell us anything about the universe, and he maintains that humans are naturally disposed to being kindly and sympathetic toward one another. Seeing the human being as a creature who is very much at home in the world, Hume himself is little inclined to try to change it.

John Dewey brings us up to the twentieth century. Strongly influenced by Darwin's theory of evolution, he sees the human being as a creature who must constantly meet the demands of a changing environment. Nothing, either in physical nature or in human culture, is fixed. Humans are gifted over all other creatures with a problem-solving intelligence. How to develop this intelligence and to use it most effectively in the advancement of humankind is Dewey's constant theme.

Although each chapter is essentially self-contained, the six chapters taken together present a varied display. Human nature is as manifold as our ways of seeing it. These six ways are well established in the history of culture. They are offered not only as models but also as intellectual resources to help us clarify our own vision.

## Suggestions for Discussion and Study

1. What do you think is the major difference between humans and other creatures?
2. What are the three kinds of human nature, and what mode of study does each inspire?
3. What is a complete image of human nature?
4. Why is the Darwinian image of human nature a partial image?
5. What are some of the principles of *ideal* conduct you believe you've inherited from your elders?
6. Before proceeding to the following chapters, write a personal essay in which you respond to Kant's three questions of existence. Keep this essay for future reference. After you've studied how the six main thinkers presented in this book answer the same questions, go back to your original essay. How would you now firm it up or change it?
7. What person whom you have known personally has had the greatest influence on your life? What historical person has had the greatest influence on your life? Can you specify the nature of these influences? How do these influences figure in to what you think a human being *ought* to be?

# Further Reading

Boulding, Kenneth E. *The Image: Knowledge in Life and Society*. Ann Arbor:
The University of Michigan Press, Ann Arbor Paperbacks, 1963.
Applies the concept of the image to various aspects of modern
culture.

Eiseley, Loren. *Darwin's Century: Evolution and the Man Who Discovered It*.
New York: Doubleday & Co., Inc., Anchor Books, 1961. Places the
rise of evolutionary concepts in the broad context of Western
intellectual history.

James, William. *The Will to Believe, and Other Essays in Popular Philosophy*.
New York: Longmans, Green & Co., 1897. Explores relationships
between belief and philosophical understanding.

# Notes

1. Gardner Murphy, "Three Kinds of Human Nature," in *Human Nature: Theories, Conjectures, and Descriptions*, ed. John J. Mitchell. (Metuchen, N.J.: The Scarecrow Press, Inc., 1972), pp. 78–88.
2. Arthur O. Lovejoy, *Reflections on Human Nature* (Baltimore: Johns Hopkins Press, 1961), pp. 13–14.
3. Ibid., p. 13.
4. Karl Jaspers, *Philosophy for Everyman: A Short Course in Philosophical Thinking* (New York: Harcourt, Brace & World, Inc., 1967), p. 34.
5. Hans Vaihinger, *The Philosophy of 'As If,'* trans. C. K. Ogden (London: Routledge & Kegan Paul, Ltd., 1965), pp. 7–8.
6. Ibid., pp. 42–50.
7. Sören Kierkegaard, "The Journals," in *A Kierkegaard Anthology*, ed. Robert Bretall (Princeton, N.J.: Princeton University Press, 1946). p. 5.
8. Immanuel Kant, *Kant's Introduction to Logic and his Essay on the Mistaken Subtility of the Four Figures*, trans. Thomas Kingmill Abbott (New York: Philosophical Library, 1963), pp. 14–15.
9. Aristotle, *The Works of Aristotle*, J. A. Smith and W. D. Ross, eds.: *Historia Animalium*, trans. D'Arcy Wentworth Thompson (Oxford: Clarendon Press, 1949), book 6: paragraphs 588b-589a.
10. Charles Darwin, *The Origin of Species by Means of Natural Selection and the Descent of Man and Selection in Relation to Sex* (New York: The Modern Library, 1936), p. 920.
11. Charles Darwin, as quoted from original manuscripts, in Howard E. Gruber and Paul H. Barrett, *Darwin on Man: A Psychological Study of Scientific Creativity* (New York: E. P. Dutton & Co., Inc., 1974), p. 213.
12. Ibid.

13. Charles Darwin, *The Autobiography of Charles Darwin, 1809–1882 (With original omissions restored)* ed. Nora Barlow (London: Collins, 1958), p. 92.
14. Vaihinger, op. cit., p. 43.
15. Jean-Paul Sartre, "Existentialism Is a Humanism," trans. Philip Mariet, in *The Existentialist Tradition: Selected Writings*, ed. Nino Langiulli (Garden City, N.Y.: Doubleday & Co., Inc., Anchor Books, 1971), p. 399.
16. Ruth Benedict, *Patterns of Culture* (New York: Mentor Books, 1950), p. 33.

# ▪1▪

# CONFUCIUS
## and the image of
# THE INDIVIDUAL
# IN SOCIETY

# Cultural Background

Chinese culture is at least four thousand years, its origins being couched in legend. The earliest historical records of this culture are related to the Shang dynasty, which was overthrown in 1122 B.C. by the Chou people. The Chou dynasty that was established by this conquering people lasted for the next 900 years, till 221 B.C., as a feudal system that covered a considerable portion of North China.

Ancestor worship, a main element of Shang religion, was carried over into the Chou dynasty. The Shang kings traced their line of descent from Shang Ti, who was recognized as the founder-ancestor of the race. Shang Ti's will was sought in all matters of political life. When a king died, he went to heaven to join his great ancestor, while his eldest son took his place as king and chief intercessor with past ancestors. In Shang religion, therefore, we find the veneration of ancestors and of things traditional that played so strong a role in the thought of Confucius.

At the beginning of the Chou dynasty, whose main rulers were King Wen, King Wu, and the Duke of Chou, the inherited feudal system worked agreeably as a form of government. (Confucius, centuries later, looked upon the early days of the Chou dynasty as a kind of Golden Age.)

From their seat of power in the Yellow River valley, the early Chou kings collected tribute from lesser lords in the surrounding regions. The feudal lords governed their local territories with a great deal of autonomy so long as they paid the required tribute to the kings, kept the peace, and provided soldiers to help the kings maintain political stability in time of need.

But gradually the feudal lords became increasingly independent. By the time of Confucius in the sixth century B.C., China was divided into a multitude of small feudal states, which were constantly at war with each other or the barbarian tribes who threatened the Chinese people on all sides. The kings of the Chou dynasty had lost their power to the more powerful feudal lords, who in turn were weakened by struggles among themselves.

As the feudalistic system declined in the Chou dynasty, there was great social upheaval. Throughout much of the history of the dynasty there were two basic classes of people: the ruling class, whose powers were inherited, and the common class, who lived largely at the behest of the rulers with little hope of social advancement.

Gradually, a third class called *shih* ("knights") emerged. These were sons of the aristocratic ruling class who by rights should have received lands of their own and positions in government. But in a government that was rife with corruption and disorder, there was little place for them. Hence, these knights were either reduced to poverty, or they set forth to make their way in the world, using to advantage their education. Only certain occupations were open to them: working in the service of a ruler, serving as military officers, becoming merchants and traders, or becoming scholars who wandered from state to state selling their services to the highest bidder. It was into this class of able, ambitious men who could claim noble descent that Confucius was born.

## Biography

Confucius is the Latinized name of K'ung Fu-tzu, which means K'ung the Master. He was born in the province of Lu (now Shantung) in 551 B.C., and died there in 479. As with many great historical figures, the biography of Confucius is highly embellished, making it difficult to separate the man from the myth. The main source of information about Confucius' life and teachings, however, lies in two major bodies of literature that the Confucian canon comprises: the Five Classics and the Four Books.

The Five Classics of Confucianism are works from the past that Confucius had a hand in editing and that profoundly shaped his own thought. They include the *I Ching* ("Changes"), a manual of divination; the *Shu Ching* ("History"), a collection of documents ascribed to kings of the Shang and early Chou dynasties; the *Li Chi* ("Rites"), a compendium of ritual; the *Shih Ching* ("Songs"), a collection of ancient poetry; and the *Ch'un Ch'iu* ("*Spring and Autumn Annals of the State of Lu*"), a chronicle of Confucius' native state (a Classic sometimes ascribed to Confucius himself).

Alongside these Classics exist the Four Books of Confucianism, works written after the death of the Master that focus and enlarge upon his life and teaching. They include the *Ta Hsueh* ("*Great Learning*"), dealing with the Confucian system of education; the *Chung Yung* ("*Doctrine of the Mean*"), dealing with the Confucian theme of moderation; *Mencius*, a collection of sayings that bears the name of Confucius' great successor; and the *Lun Yu* ("*Analects*"), a collection of notes kept by his disciples on the Master's discourses. Of the books written or compiled after Confucius' death, the *Analects* gives the most reliable picture of him as an actual person (and we will rely on it in considering his ideology).

When Confucius was a mere infant, his father died, leaving the mother to rear the child. Their circumstances were anything but affluent. When Confucius was questioned in later life why he, a scholar, was experienced in so many mundane affairs, he explained, "When I was young I was in humble circumstances; that is why I have many practical accomplishments in regard to simple, everyday accomplishments."[1]

Toward the end of his life, Confucius succinctly described his own career.

> At fifteen I set my heart upon learning. At thirty, I had planted my feet firm upon the ground. At forty, I no longer suffered from perplexities. At fifty, I knew what were the biddings of Heaven. At sixty, I heard them with docile ear. At seventy, I could follow the dictates of my own heart; for what I desired no longer overstepped the boundaries of right.[2]

This sketchy chronology can be filled in with details that owe a great deal to Confucian lore.

As a young man Confucius married, became a father, and worked for a nobleman in the state of Lu as an overseer in charge of the granary, oxen, and sheep. But he was primarily a man of scholarly ambition who managed to acquire a strong grasp of the classical learning of his day.

In his early thirties he was already known as a teacher of *Li* ("*ritual*"), the rules of propriety or proper conduct that serve in traditional Chinese thought as the basis of civilization. His growing reputation as a teacher of broad learning, not only in ritual but also in literature and history, helped him to become established in the governmental service of the Duke of Lu. But Confucius' time was one of political intrigue. When the Duke of Lu was threatened by powerful rivals among the local nobility, he was forced to flee to a neighboring state, where Confucius joined him. When Confucius was able to return to the state of Lu, he spent the next fifteen years perfecting his studies and expanding his reputation as a teacher.

At age fifty, Confucius returned to political life, where he attained a position of some importance in the government. In spite of this position, however, he was unable to affect the necessary political and social reforms that he envisioned, and he resigned his post after five years. Leaving the state of Lu, he traveled widely through China for the next twelve years with a group of his disciples, allegedly seeking a position of political influence elsewhere, but without success.

In 484 B.C., when he was sixty-seven, Confucius returned to Lu, where he devoted the last six years of his life to teaching a growing number of disciples what it means to be properly human. By Confucius' own standards, his life had been a failure. The political and social conditions of China were as wretched as when he had begun his career. Nonetheless, he had commended a way of life that was to affect profoundly the lives of men and women in the centuries after him.

## Confucius on What Can I Know?

The *Analects* is not simple to grasp, even in reputable translation. Like the New Testament, it demands to be read in its own special way, in fairly long extracts, for then patterns of meaning emerge that aren't obvious if we read passages in isolation. Some background reading is important, too, and here Arthur Waley's fine introduction to his translation of the *Analects* is helpful. In paraphrasing Confucius' ideas, we'll attempt to represent them accurately, but only the readers who undertake a patient rereading of the text for themselves will begin to get the *feel* of Confucian thought.

Confucius was a thinker whose entire philosophy was based on a sense of mission. It was his task to save Chinese society from the anarchy that beset it: internecine wars, vast disparities between the rich and the poor, inadequate education, and the lack of accepted standards pertaining to moral conduct. The China of Confucius' day was marked by a dog-eat-dog mentality that can be described in the words of a modern poet, William Butler Yeats, who saw this same mentality prevailing in his own day.

> Things fall apart; the center cannot hold;
> Mere anarchy is loosed upon the world.[3]

The main philosophical question that Confucius directed at the social situation of his day was how human beings, who are driven by individual, often selfish desires, can learn to live together. For him, social harmony depended upon human beings having a common sense of tradition. The major task Confucius set for himself, therefore, was that of learning, and in turn teaching others, about the great traditions of China's past.

Confucius identified China's Golden Age of social harmony with the early Chou dynasty, especially the leadership of the Duke of Chou. It was tradition, Confucius maintained, that had produced this Golden Age. Because cultural values were finely conceived, firmly in place, and widely respected, people lived well by them. Even at the risk of idolizing China's past, Confucius envied it and wished to imitate it in his own time. As tradition held the secret to life then, so must it hold the secret now.

It was not just the specifics of tradition that Confucius wanted to impress on those whom he taught, however, but the secret of *Tao* (pronounced "dow"), which he knew tradition to embrace. The knowledge that is most worth having, Confucius maintained, is knowledge of the *Tao*.

The notion of *Tao* (literally meaning "the Path" or "the Way") had its roots in the religious heritage of China. But Confucius, through his interpretation of tradition, applied *Tao* to a broad range of secular matters: for example, the appropriate way to run a government or to manage a family or to conduct one's personal affairs. The Confucian notion of the Way points to a rightness of things that penetrates to the very heart of the universe, which Confucius refers to reverentially as "the will of Heaven."[4] For Confucius, the Way of Heaven is an objective order of value that, when adhered to, results in the Way of human life. To be wise is to follow the Way one ought to follow because it is laid down by the Way of Heaven. Thus, when the Master says, "In the morning, hear the Way; in the evening, die content,"[5] he is referring to a deferential, correct attitude toward that which is unconditionally the Good in itself.

The Confucian notion of knowledge of the Way raises the question of transmission. To Western ears, at least, the idea of the Way of Heaven connotes the supernatural. But Confucius was not a thinker who relied on supernatural revelation or inspiration. His disciples noted that the Master was unwilling to discourse about the "ways of Heaven."[6] From Confucius' point of view, the study of tradition as contained in sage writings of the past was the chief means by which knowledge of the Way is transmitted. For him, knowledge of the Way was based on the study of history; in documents of the distant past, particularly the early Chou dynasty, Confucius believed it was possible to recover the Way in the present. As an interpreter of the past, Confucius was a perpetuator of tradition and a teacher of the knowledge of the Way to his own time.

## Confucius on What Ought I to Do?

What exactly did Confucius teach as the essence of tradition to those disciples who studied with him? Before we answer this question, we need to understand who those disciples were and what educational goals Confucius conceived for them.

Confucius wanted to extend education beyond the aristocratic class, opening the doors to everybody who was willing to learn. His aim of democracy in education, however, did not extend to women for the main reason that women did not control power in government, and Confucius was intent on educating persons who would serve in government circles. His disciples, or students, were men whom he sought to train in "the Way of the true gentleman,"[7] men who possessed a certain quality of human nature. He assumed his students would attain positions of responsibility and trust because of their sincerity, loyalty, uprightness, and obedience to the dictates of conscience and the promptings of a humane, just mind.

In discussing the Confucian idea of education, then, we must use such terms as "true gentleman," "true manhood," or "superior man," for it was in such terms that Confucius thought and spoke. It should be clear to the modern reader, however, that the educational goals Confucius sought for men apply equally to women.

The enhancement of human nature through education is not a privilege of gender.

Confucian education demands that an individual bring his or her own character or nature into harmony with certain ideas laid down by the Way of Heaven, the unconditional Good. They are discerned in those venerable traditions that have produced harmony in the social order of the past. For Confucius, at least five of these ideals are eminently worthy of pursuit as the essence of the Way. In response to the question What ought I to do? Confucius would have answered, Seek refinement in *Jen* ("goodness"), in *Chun-tzu* ("noble-mindedness"), in *Li* ("propriety"), in *Te* ("moral force"), and in *Wen* ("the arts of peace"). Let's consider each of these ideals in detail, for they stand at the center of the Confucian idea of education and the Master's image of human nature.

### Jen, or Goodness

The term *Jen* refers to an ultimately desirable condition in human relationships. It's a term that translators have variously defined as humaneness, human-heartedness, benevolence, love, charity, and compassion. But goodness perhaps best captures the overall sense of *Jen*. The simplest description of goodness is that given by Confucius in response to his disciple Fan Ch'ih: the person who possesses goodness "loves men."[8] Later, the Master indicates that goodness may be broken down into various components.

> Tzu-chang asked Master K'ung about Goodness. Master K'ung said, He who could put the Five into practice everywhere under Heaven would be Good. Tzu-chang begged to hear what these were. The Master said, Courtesy, breadth, good faith, diligence and clemency. 'He who is courteous is not scorned, he who is broad wins the multitude, he who is of good faith is trusted by the people, he who is diligent succeeds in all he undertakes, he who is clement can get service from the people.'[9]

In Confucius' view, goodness is the greatest, the summation, of all human excellences, or virtues. Based on a profound belief in the universal dignity of human life, it involves both a respect for oneself and a feeling of humanity toward others. The Master admitted, however, that it was an ideal so difficult to attain that he had never known it to be realized in any living person. It belonged primarily to the sage scholars and rulers of old, men whose lives were worthy of imitation as examples of human perfectibility.

All human beings act according to their nature, Confucius maintains, but a person's nature, though bestowed by the Way of Heaven, is in an unperfected condition. Goodness is emblematic of human nature in its perfected condition. While goodness may be all but impossible for the human being to achieve, it must nevertheless be claimed as the goal toward which one strives. There is thus a teleological, or goal-oriented, dimension in Confucian education. What the human being should be concerned with first of all is the increase of goodness in his or her life.

> Has anyone ever managed to do Good with his whole might even as long as the space of a single day? I think not. Yet I for my part have never seen anyone give up such an attempt because he had not the *strength* to go on. It may well have happened, but I for my part have never seen it.[10]

With these words the Master indicates that if a person fails to increase goodness in his or her own life, then it's the person's will, not the Way itself, that is wanting.

### Chun-tzu, or Noble-Mindedness

The second Confucian ideal that belongs to the essence of the Way is *Chun-tzu*. Since goodness seemed so far beyond the reach of ordinary mortals, Confucius concentrated upon fashioning true gentlemen, an ideal he assumed all dedicated men might reasonably strive after. Originally, the term *Chun-tzu* referred to a member of the ruling, as opposed to the common, class. But Confucius dropped the idea of class distinction. *Chun-tzu* refers to any man who aspires to the virtue of goodness and in so doing cultivates a certain quality of noble-mindedness. "There are three things," Confucius observes,

that a gentleman, in following the Way, places above all
the rest: from every attitude, every gesture that he employs
he must remove all trace of violence or arrogance; every
look that he composes in his face must betoken good faith;
from every word that he utters, from every intonation, he
must remove all trace of coarseness or impropriety.[11]

Here we have a description of the gentleman as an individual
of personal poise and grace. But Confucius also stressed the noble-
mindedness of the gentleman in his concern for others.

Tzu-lu asked about the qualities of a true gentleman. The
Master said, He cultivates in himself the capacity to be
diligent in his tasks. Tzu-lu said, Can he not go further than
that? The Master said, He cultivates in himself the capacity
to ease the lot of other people. Tzu-lu said, Can he not go
further than that? The Master said, He cultivates in himself
the capacity to ease the lot of the whole populace.[12]

The gentleman who emerges in Confucian thought is an
individual of perfect address who knows his own mind. Because
he focuses his thought and actions upon the Way he is able to
withstand the storms of life, where men of lesser perfection would
be overwhelmed. It's only the individual who is noble-minded,
Confucius assumes, who can provide the basic human stuff of
culture. "Culture cannot make gentlemen,"[13] Confucius insists,
but gentlemen can make culture. On them the whole course of
civilized society depends.

## Li, or Propriety

The third ideal that Confucius sees as pivotal in pursuit of the
Way is *Li*. The Way of the gentleman is long and the life of the
individual short. One of the most important insights of Confucian
education is that the wisdom of the past is accumulative. It's not
out of mere modesty that Confucius says of himself, "I have
'transmitted what was taught to me without making up anything
of my own.' I have been faithful to and loved the Ancients."[14]
Rather, it's out of the conviction that faithfulness to the Ancients
is the key to personal wisdom and growth in the present.

This whole idea of faithfulness to the Ancients and the ways of tradition is captured in the ideal of *Li*. This term is variously translated as ritual, rules, ceremony, good manners, or good behavior. Perhaps we'll come closest to the mark if we adhere to the idea of propriety.

Originally, *Li* referred to religious rites, especially the formalities attending acts of religious sacrifice. In ancient China, however, religious and secular activities were not widely separated, and long before Confucius' time the idea of propriety concerning religious activities was extended to include propriety in secular activities as well. The whole life of the gentleman, in Confucius' view, is to be conducted with propriety. The Master says to one of his disciples, Jan Jung, "Behave when away from home as though you were in the presence of an important guest. Deal with the common people as though you were officiating at an important sacrifice."[15] What Confucius is commending here is a practiced attitude of deference and decorum in relation to others. At other times, he's quite exact about the rules of such decorum.

> If he [the gentleman] is ill and his prince comes to see him, he has himself laid with his head to the East with his Court robes thrown over him and his sash drawn across the bed. When the prince commands his presence he goes straight to the palace without waiting for his carriage to be yoked.[16]

The Confucian idea of propriety may strike the modern read-er as artificial and constrictive. But for Confucius, whose age was marked by a rampant sense of disorder, it was the means by which relations among persons could be formalized at the levels of family and state and the social order regulated. Propriety afforded a standard of behavior within which actions were motivated by a pattern of cooperative thought rather than personal passions. The practice of propriety for the Confucian gentleman, therefore, involves a knowledge of ancient social traditions and the ability to realize them in current circumstances. "A gentleman who . . . knows how to submit . . . to the restraints of ritual [propriety]," Confucius asserts, "is not likely . . . to go far wrong."[17]

## Te, or Morality

*Te* is the fourth crucial ideal in following the Way. Confucius realizes that goodness becomes embodied in society not simply through observance of propriety but also through the morality of the individual human. *Te* means moral force; the moral individual is, for Confucius, the hub of the universe. Speaking of the character of the ruler, he says, "He who rules by moral force . . . is like the pole-star, which remains in its place while all the lesser stars do homage to it."[18] Everything in the well-ordered society that Confucius envisions depends on the cultivation of personal integrity, in the honest matching of deeds with thoughts, in the giving and keeping of one's word, in living by example as well as by precept, and in being exactly what one gives the appearance of being. Moral force, in the Confucian sense, involves living by a standard that in both tone and intention correlates with the Golden Rule of the Bible: "Never do to others what you would not like them to do to you."[19]

## Wen, or the Arts of Peace

The last major ideal in the Confucian scheme of education is *Wen*. In principle, Confucius was not opposed to war. He knew that at times physical force must be used by moral persons to prevent themselves from being enslaved by aggressors. Nonetheless, he believed that the Way of the gentleman lay in the cultivation of *Wen*, the arts of peace, as opposed to the arts of war.

Confucius regards art, poetry, and music as powerful civilizing influences. "Little ones," he says to his disciples, "Why is it that none of you study the *Songs*? For the *Songs* will help you to incite people's emotions, to observe their feelings, to keep company, to express your grievances."[20] Confucius himself is known to have especially loved music and to have been committed to playing the zither and singing. Indeed, music so strongly impressed him on one occasion that, after hearing a particular musical performance, he did not "know the taste of meat" for three months. "I did not picture to myself," the Master exclaimed, "that any music existed which could reach such perfection as this."[21]

The Confucian emphasis on the aesthetic aspect of life is based on the assumption that the individual who values and practices the arts knows something of the harmony and beauty of the Way of Heaven. Confucius trusts that the arts, in their intrinsic connection to the Way, have the power to assuage base passions and to awaken noble passions. So, in urging his disciples to become proficient in the arts of peace, he is trying to put them in touch with a main source of inspiration in the attainment of human perfection. For Confucius, the arts of peace provide a window on that absolute perfection, the Way, which is behind and beneath all things.

To recapitulate, therefore, Confucius' response to the question What ought I to do? is located in the five main ideals he taught to his disciples: goodness, noble-mindedness, propriety, moral force, and the arts of peace. As he studied tradition, Confucius saw these five ideals standing forth as the essence of the Way of Heaven and as the essence of human nature. Held before the Confucian follower, they afford the standards by which the individual's struggle in the Way and the fulfillment of his or her own nature is to be measured.

## Confucius on for What Can I Hope?

If Confucian thought as we have thus far described it seems primarily ethical and social in character, it's because the Master did not often concern himself with matters that did not have a practical human aspect. When the disciple Tzu-lu questioned him about death, for example, he said, "Till you know about the living, how are you to know about the dead?"[22] In the same conversation, when Tzu-lu asked him what was proper in the service of the spirits and the gods, the Master responded, "Till you have learnt to serve men, how can you serve ghosts?"[23]

These quotations afford a clue to Confucius' basic religious outlook: he is concerned more with the living than the dead, with morality than worship, with human order than divine order. "Heaven does not speak," Confucius proclaims, "yet the four seasons run their course thereby."[24] The attitude reflected in this remark is consistent with that of a deist, i.e., one who acknowledges a divine force in the universe but who sees this force as manifesting itself predominantly in the orderly workings of nature. Confucius' religious outlook is perhaps best summarized in the words of the scholar of Chinese thought H. G. Creel: "Confucius thought of Heaven as an impersonal ethical force, a cosmic counterpart of the ethical sense in man, a guarantee that somehow there is sympathy with man's sense of right in the very nature of the universe."[25]

The hope that Confucius holds out as the main goal of human existence is profoundly this-worldly, as opposed to other-worldly, in character. He assumes it's possible for right-thinking, right-acting people to imitate the Way of Heaven in an earthly state. Confucius himself does not give us a picture of his ideal state, it having been formulated several years after his death in a passage that is attributed to him.

> When the Great Way was practiced, the world was shared by all alike. The worthy and the able were promoted to office and men practiced good faith and lived in affection. Therefore they did not regard as parents only their own parents, or as sons only their own sons. The aged found a fitting close to their lives, the robust their proper employment; the young were provided with an upbringing and the widow and widower, the orphaned and the sick, with proper care. Men had their tasks and women their hearths. They hated to see goods lying about in waste, yet they did not hoard them for themselves; they disliked the thought that their energies were not fully used, yet they used them not for private ends. Therefore all evil plotting was prevented and thieves and rebels did not arise, so that people could leave their outer gates unbolted. This was the age of Grand Unity.[26]

Confucius' "Grand Unity" (the ideal state, in other words) envisions a minimum of human suffering. Members of families are concerned for the welfare of one another, and the state takes on the complexion of a huge extended family, wherein things are well governed and ordered from top to bottom. Peace and order thrive because the state realizes in practice, at the level of the general population, that virtue which epitomizes human nature, or goodness. To live in such a state, Confucius assumes, is the highest goal of human striving and happiness.

The ideal state that Confucius envisioned was not realized in his own lifetime, nor has it been realized in China or any other political state since the Master's death. But in the final analysis, this historical failure does not diminish the value of Confucius' teachings to the world at large. Wherever men and women continue to believe that the hope for humankind lies in the attainment of wisdom, the exercise of discipline, and the practice of benevolence, there the spirit of Confucius abides.

## Implications of the Confucian Image of Human Nature

Ever since the ancient Greeks defined the human being as a rational animal, it's been commonly assumed in Western thought that an individual comes equipped, in a manner of speaking, with his or her nature complete, endowed at birth with certain attributes that make him or her the kind of creature he or she is. It's hard to overestimate the influence this birthright theory of human nature has had within Western tradition. One extension of it is the principle of individualism, or the belief that the most important fact about the human being is one's individuality—his or her particular mind and body, desires and rights, life and destiny.

To be sure, in a sense every human is an individual at birth and therefore owes himself or herself a certain responsibility because of what and who he or she is. But after we have acknowledged this responsibility, we're bound to go a step further and acknowledge that most of our responsibilities are social. Not only is each human a unique being, each is also a member of a family, a state, a culture. As individuals, we cannot separate ourselves from the demands and influences that the social structure brings to bear upon us. If there should be a worldwide natural disaster or a nuclear holocaust that destroyed every human being except one, the life of that survivor—deprived of a social structure—would be so impoverished that the idea of responsibility to himself or herself would be virtually meaningless.

No thinker has seen more clearly than Confucius that human beings are not simply born with those attributes that constitute their nature. Rather, they acquire the fullness of their nature through the dynamic process of interacting with other humans.

The Confucian final test for any society is whether it produces individuals who behave with dignity and self-respect and are eager to do good in relation to others.

But if a society doesn't meet this test, we might ask, if it's unhealthy in the sense that those qualities of human nature are generally wanting, then is there any hope for realizing them? Confucius' answer—the health of a society rests in the hands of those individuals, almost certainly in the minority, who perceive the Way or the Good and are bound together by a common loyalty to the Good—furnishes the key to much of his philosophical message.

The Confucian idea of loyalty is more than a sentiment existing within the recesses of the mind. It's an active giving of the self on the part of the individual to a larger life. The individual who does no more than profess an abstract loyalty to the goal does not fulfill his or her role as a member of society. To fulfill that role he or she must perform deeds that have a definite relevance to, and are an outward expression of, the professed loyalty. In this way a society, though it depends heavily on the ideal spirit of understanding, reaps health in a world of time and change. It lives in and through the steady efforts of its members who are committed to realizing through their own lives the common good for which the society exists.

What the Confucian ideal of society asks foremost is a sense of selflessness on the part of the individual in the name of all. It promises that this sense of selflessness will be rewarded by a healthful society in which the individual can flourish and realize the fullness of his or her nature. If, for even one generation, a society were totally without individuals who placed the common good before their private interests, that society would disintegrate, for it would lack that very spirit required to bind it together.

As an Eastern thinker, Confucius challenges us to reevaluate some of our basic Western principles. One of these principles, as we have indicated, is individualism. Could it be that the principle of individualism has assumed exaggerated importance in the tradition of Western thought?

At least one modern thinker, Eric Fromm, thinks this is exactly the case. Individualism, he maintains, has come to manifest itself in Western life as "narcissism," a term he uses to cover all forms of vanity in individuals—self-admiration, self-satisfaction, and self-glorification—and all forms of parochialism in groups—ethnic or racial prejudice and political fanaticism. "Narcissism," in other words, is Fromm's metaphor for the "asocial"[27] individualism he sees everywhere in Western life, undermining cooperation, defying benevolence, and thwarting the search for wider loyalties.

Perhaps the sting of Fromm's judgment is tolerable only because it contains the antidote of truth. One lesson we stand to learn from the Confucian image of human nature is just how comprehensive our humanity is. Is it possible to really know ourselves, to be aware of the richness of our nature, if we insist on saying "I" without also saying "we"?

# Suggestions for Discussion and Study

1. The Confucian concept of the Way assumes an objective order of value in the universe itself. C. S. Lewis speaks of the Way, or the *Tao*, in the following manner:

   It is the doctrine of objective value, the belief that certain attitudes are really true, and others really false, to the kind of thing the universe is and the kind of things we are. Those who know the *Tao* can hold that to call children delightful or old men venerable is not simply to record a psychological fact about our own parental or filial emotions at the moment, but to recognize a quality which *demands* a certain response from us whether we make it or not. I myself do not enjoy the society of small children: because I speak from within the *Tao* I recognize this as a defect in myself—just as a man may have to recognize that he is tone deaf or colour blind (*The Abolition of Man: How Education Develops Man's Sense of Morality* [New York: Macmillan Publishing Co., Inc., 1978], p. 29).

   Lewis is a modern thinker who assents to the Confucian concept of the *Tao*. According to him, our emotions and opinions are always to be tested against an objective, universally valid standard of value. Can you give any reasons for believing such an objective standard exists? Is the *Tao* real?

2. Confucius regards the early Chou Dynasty as the period of "Grand Unity," when Chinese society existed as a harmonious

whole. Such a period of utopian harmony may never have actually existed, but it was nevertheless a vision that Confucius pursued. Is there any period in the history of the United States of America that corresponds to the Confucian vision of "Grand Unity"?

3. What would it be like in the life of an ordinary citizen to spend even one day in a society where the "Grand Unity" prevailed?

4. Confucius contends that goodness is the absolute goal of personal striving. It is the preeminent virtue, practically impossible to attain. Is his idea of goodness unrealistically high? Is there a sense of perfectionism in the Confucian ideal of morality that frustrates ordinary human striving?

5. Confucius believes that the life of the gentleman, or the person who aspires toward goodness, will have a positive influence on those persons with whom he comes in contact. In short, he assumes that the power of goodness is attractive and will cause persons who see it exemplified to respect and imitate it. But isn't there such a thing in human nature as a willingness to imitate evil rather than good? Does Confucius give adequate recognition to the darker dispositions of the human heart?

6. Life in modern China has experienced upheavals because of the dynamic impact of the West. With the entire structure of Chinese society shaken and reevaluated in light of modern knowledge, Confucianism has fallen into certain disfavor. Speculate on the main reasons for this disfavor on the basis of what you understand about modern ideas of progress.

7. What do you find to be most compelling in the Confucian image of human nature?

# Further Reading

Creel, H. G. *Confucius and the Chinese Way.* New York: Harper & Row, Publishers, Harper Torchbooks, 1960. A thorough study of Confucius' life and thought and his impact on Chinese life down to the twentieth century.

Latourette, Kenneth Scott. *The Chinese: Their History and Culture.* New York: The Macmillan Co., 1962. A comprehensive historical approach.

Lewis, C. S. *The Abolition of Man: How Education Develops Man's Sense of Morality.* New York: Macmillan Publishing Co., Inc., 1955. An application of the Confucian concept of the *Tao* to modern morality.

Spiegelberg, Frederic. *Living Religions of the World.* Englewood Cliffs, N.J.: Prentice-Hall, Inc., 1956. Discusses Confucius as both a religious and philosophical thinker within the context of the Chinese worldview.

Waley, Arthur. *Three Ways of Thought in Ancient China.* New York: Doubleday & Co., Doubleday Anchor Books, n.d. A comparison and contrast of three schools of philosophical thought in ancient Chinese culture: the Taoist, the Confucianist, and the Realist.

# Notes

1. *The Analects of Confucius,* trans. and annot. Arthur Waley (New York: Random House, Vintage Books, 1938), p. 139. (All quotations from the *Analects* are from this edition.)
2. Ibid., p. 88.
3. William Butler Yeats, "The Second Coming," *The Collected Poems of W. B. Yeats* (New York: The Macmillan Co., 1957), stanza 1, lines 3–4.
4. Waley, op. cit., p. 189.
5. Ibid., p. 103.
6. Ibid., p. 110.
7. Ibid., pp. 110–111.
8. Ibid., p. 169.
9. Ibid., pp. 210–211.
10. Ibid., p. 103.
11. Ibid., p. 133.
12. Ibid., p. 191.
13. Ibid., p. 164.
14. Ibid., p. 123.
15. Ibid., p. 162.
16. Ibid., p. 150.
17. Ibid., p. 121.
18. Ibid., p. 88.
19. Ibid., p. 198.
20. Ibid., p. 212.
21. Ibid., p. 125.
22. Ibid., p. 155.
23. Ibid.
24. Ibid., p. 214.
25. H. G. Creel, *Confucius and the Chinese Way* (New York: Harper & Row, Publishers, Harper Torchbooks, 1960). p. 117.

26. *Sources of Chinese Tradition*, 2 vols., comps. Theodore De Bary, Wing-Tsit Chan, Burton Watson (New York: Columbia University Press, 1971), I: 176.
27. Eric Fromm, *Heart of Man* (New York: Harper & Row, Publishers, Harper Colophon Books, 1980), pp. 66–73.

# ·2·

# SOPHOCLES
## and the image of
# TRAGIC HEROISM

# Cultural Background

No century in the history of humankind was more momentous than the sixth century B.C. A number of thinkers whose names are associated with the dawning of universal religions emerged in that century: Confucius and Lao-Tzu in China; Buddha in India; Isaiah in Israel; and Thales and Pythagoras in Greece. It was also the century of Cyrus, the founder of the Persian Empire, the first example of politics on a grand scale and the best organized political structure before the Roman Empire.

Karl Jaspers has suggested that we augment this period of our attention to the six hundred years from 800 B.C. to 200 B.C. and call it the "axial period."[1] The term axial connotes a major turning point in the history of human development. During this period, Jaspers maintains, a type of human being emerged whose structure of existence differed from that of human beings who had gone before.

The propensity for rational thought basically distinguished the human being of the axial period from his or her predecessors. Reason is distinct from other modes of thought such as remembering, daydreaming, intuiting, and dreaming. Reason is the mental capacity whereby we draw inferences and use known facts to arrive at new facts. The human being of the axial period began to apply reason as the dominant mode of thought.

For example, no longer was this new type of human being content to comprehend life poetically, in terms of stories about the intermingled doings of gods and mortals. Rather, the axial human being tried to comprehend life rationally, in terms of discursive descriptions of natural phenomena. Ancient Greek culture, with its contributions to mathematics, science, art, architecture, literature, and philosophy, is the main glory of human accomplishment within the axial period. This culture represents the first great blossoming of the rationalistic spirit that has characterized Western thought up to our own day.

The Greek epic poet Homer, who wrote around 750 B.C., stands on the threshold of the axial period. In reading his *Iliad* and *Odyssey*, we perceive that he assumes the actuality of the Olympian gods, as well as the heroes of the Trojan War, just as many persons in the Judeo-Christian tradition have assumed the actuality of Adam and Eve and Noah, as spoken of in Genesis. The

Homeric stories provided the basic material for sculptors and poets of Greek culture and profoundly influenced the ancient Greek vision of life.

The last commanding literary expressions of the Homeric Greek vision appeared in the plays of Aeschylus and Sophocles. A weakening of this vision appeared in the plays of Euripides and Aristophanes, in the Sophist philosophers, and in Socrates. When Socrates was accused at his trial of disbelieving in the gods that the Athenian state believed in, the claim was no doubt accurate. Socrates was not, at bottom, an irreligious person, but he did subject the traditional religious views of his day to intense rational scrutiny.

For Socrates, it was more important to focus on the life of humans than on the life of the Olympian gods, and he accordingly placed human life at the center of philosophical inquiry. He came to understand his vocation as a philosopher in connection with Delphi, the town of the oracles of Apollo. Socrates interpreted the precept of the oracle of Delphi, "Know thyself," to mean that the knowledge of one's nature is the true end of life. "Life without . . . examination," Socrates insisted, "is not worth living,"[2] because it's only through knowing ourselves—the kind of creatures we are and what we are capable of—that we learn how to fulfill ourselves.

Reason, in Socrates' estimation, was the main instrument in the fulfillment of ourselves. He assumed that nothing happens by accident either in nature or in human life. Things are shot through with connections to the extent that all events and actions involve implications, even though some of them are hard to see. Rationality, as Socrates applied it to human life, involved the anticipation of consequences of our actions and the governing of our actions in light of those possible consequences. He believed that through reason the human being has the power to fashion his or her own existence and to attain a state of well-being, or happiness.

The lives of Socrates, the philosopher, and Sophocles, the playwright, overlapped in fifth-century Athens, where both men shared and helped to shape the intellectual outlook of their day. Like his philosophical contemporary, Sophocles also recognized the need for knowing human nature. He would have agreed with Socrates that we should strive to conduct our lives along rational lines. But unlike Socrates, he was inherently skeptical about our power to do so. In his plays, Sophocles cultivates the insight that forces at work in our lives and in the universe baffle even our sincerest attempts at rationality and defy even our best attempts to attain happiness.

Sophocles' approach via the Homeric heroic tradition was much more informed than was Socrates' approach to the problem of the knowledge of one's nature. Within that tradition, individuals of greater than ordinary human size—such as Hector, Priam, Agamemnon, Achilles, and Odysseus—not only test their strengths against one another but also against the gods, whose interference in human affairs is often a main source of human suffering. In the Homeric world, humans do not discover what they are and what they are capable of through the instrument of reason. Rather, they make this discovery through personal trials of physical and spiritual suffering.

In the plays of Sophocles, we encounter individuals of Homeric magnitude who come to know their own nature primarily through personal suffering. Sophocles is credited with being the first writer in Western literature to delineate clearly the *tragic hero*: one who, in the face of opposition, makes a decision that springs from the deepest level of his being and then lives out the consequences of that decision, even to the point of personal destruction. In and through this painful process, the tragic heroes' comprehension expands and their exact human possibilities come to light. As a writer, Sophocles brings into confluence two strains of thought in Greek culture: the Socratic strain, which insists on the importance of the knowledge of one's nature, and the Homeric strain, which insists that through heroic trials and suffering this knowledge is attained.

While the age of Sophocles was especially rich in tragic literature, at least one main feature sets his work apart from that of his equally famous contemporaries, Aeschylus and Euripides. The classical scholar Werner Jaeger suggests that among these tragic writers, Sophocles is the master of "character-drawing." In reading Sophocles, we feel, even as his contemporaries must have felt, that his characters "have an independent life in the imagination apart from the stage and the actual plot in which they appear. . . . that his real flesh-and-blood men and women, with violent passions and tender emotions, proudly heroic but truly human, are like ourselves and yet noble with an incomparable dignity and remoteness."[3] We are attracted to Sophocles' characters both for their down-to-earth quality and their remoteness. We see them like ourselves, yet greatly enhanced.

## Biography

Sophocles' ninety-year life span, from 496–406 B.C., covers almost the whole of Athens' fifth-century rise to greatness and its fall. As a young man of sixteen, he took part in the celebration of the great naval victory over the Persians at Salamis, which set Athens on the road to supremacy among the Greek city states. When he died, the Athenian defeat at the hands of Sparta, at the conclusion of the long, exhaustive Peloponnesian War, was only two years off.

Sophocles, who was born in the upper class of Athenian society, was well educated, handsome (a compelling quality among the ancient Greeks), religiously devout, and widely admired by his fellow citizens. He inspired public confidence and was called upon at different stages of his career to serve as an overseer of the Athenian treasury, as an ambassador, and as a military general. Apparently, however, these duties did not conflict with his love of writing plays for the Athenian stage.

The literature of Greek tragedy emerged in conjunction with the annual Athenian festivals honoring the god Dionysus. During these festivals, writers produced their plays competitively over a period of three days. Upon several occasions, Sophocles won first place in these demanding competitions. A prolific writer, he composed, according to reasonable estimate, 123 plays, only seven of which have survived: *Ajax, Antigone, The Women of Trachis, Oedipus the King, Electra, Philoctetes,* and *Oedipus at Colonus.*

## Sophocles and the Legend of Oedipus

Sophocles wrote dramatic literature intended primarily for performance rather than for reading. When we read a play, we cannot take in more than one impression at a time as our eyes move laterally across the page. Contrast this with sitting in an audience while a play is being performed. Here we experience many impressions simultaneously: words, silences, sound effects, gestures, background music, movements across the stage, lighting, colors in the costumes and décor. All these impressions tell us something that we do not get from simply reading. Even though reading allows us to consider the contents of a play repeatedly and in depth, it is never to be preferred over seeing and hearing a play performed.

Classical Greek plays are not routinely performed in the modern theatre, though several are available on videocassettes, and it's always possible to perform them as readers' theatre, where individuals assume the roles and read directly from the text. If we're going to understand them, we're obliged to read them, even though we encounter names we cannot pronounce, we're baffled by the frequent allusions to the gods, the action seems slow and tedious, and the issues with which the plays deal seem far removed from contemporary ones. There's just no way around studiousness and the exercise of imagination if we want to understand the greatness of Greek dramatic literature.

The first word of advice on reading the Greek plays is to read them carefully, line by line, savoring the imagery and putting together the main plot. There is always some major conflict—between humans and humans, between humans and the gods—which has to be resolved. Locate that conflict as early as possible, and then follow how the playwright resolves it. Ask yourself why he resolves it in just this way. Who are the winners and losers? What does winning and losing mean to the playwright?

The second word of advice is to supplement your reading of the texts with a reputable handbook, such as *Lemprière's Classical Dictionary*, as well as with studies dealing specifically with the playwright you're pursuing. (The studies cited in Further Reading at the conclusion of this chapter are written by scholars for educated laymen, and they'll contribute greatly to the reader's understanding of Sophocles, as well as the whole of Greek drama.)

The third word of advice is to recognize that the Greek plays were not written solely for entertainment. They were calculated to show us something about the human condition. A modern counterpart to the Greek plays in this respect is the oeuvre of Norwegian playwright Henrick Ibsen (1828–1906). As you're reading, ask yourself what the playwright is trying to show us about the human condition. What image of human nature emerges in his work? With that question in mind, let's turn our thoughts specifically to Sophocles.

Sophocles was not only a magnificent poet but also a profound thinker. His image of human nature is concentrated in the legendary figure of Oedipus, Sophocles' prime dramatic symbol of human nature. The legend of Oedipus and his family was deeply embedded in the imagination of the Greek people long before Sophocles explored it in his three most celebrated plays: *Oedipus the King, Oedipus at Colonus,* and *Antigone,* which were not conceived as a trilogy. Sophocles wrote *Antigone* (the last of the plays from the point of view of story line) approximately a decade before *Oedipus the King* (the first of the plays from the point of view of story line) and approximately four decades before *Oedipus at Colonus.* Still, these plays seek to be read as a trilogy. In spite of minor discrepancies in the three plots, they afford a continual interpretation of the ordeals and destiny of Oedipus.

On the basis of *Antigone, Oedipus the King,* and *Oedipus at Colonus* (the order in which the plays were written), we'll attempt to locate Sophocles' responses to the main questions of human nature: What can I know? What ought I to do? For what can I hope? But before we begin our analysis, it's appropriate to explain the significant details of the Oedipus legend, some of which fall outside the immediate action of Sophocles' plays. The following account, woven together from Sophocles and other sources, will supply these details and provide a continuous account of the legend for the modern reader, to whom it isn't as familiar as it was to Sophocles' audience.

The legend has its dark beginnings in events prior to Oedipus' birth. When Oedipus' father, Laius, was a young man, he was received as a guest in the household of King Pelops of Corinth, where he remained for a considerable time. The ties of guest and host were among the most inviolable of human relationships, and Laius brought upon himself and his descendants a curse by kidnapping Chrysippus, the son of Pelops with whom he had fallen in love.

Later, when Laius became King of Thebes, he consulted the oracle at Delphi (a priestess who acted as the voice of Apollo) about the children who would be born to him and his wife, Jocasta. The oracle predicted that they would have a son, but that as a result of the curse of Pelops, the son would kill his father and marry his own mother.

When the son was born, therefore, Laius tried to prevent the prediction of the oracle from being realized by ordering the infant to be taken and left to die upon Mt. Cithaeron. The servant entrusted with the task went so far as to pierce the child's ankles and to tie them together, as he had been instructed to do by Laius, but he took pity on the child and gave him to a shepherd. This shepherd in turn bore the child to Polybus, King of Corinth, who, along with Queen Merope, named the child Oedipus ("swollen-foot") and reared him as their son.

One day Oedipus, now in early manhood, attended a feast at which a drunken guest taunted him, saying that Polybus and Merope were not his true parents. When news of this taunt spread throughout the city, Oedipus left Corinth in shame and asked the oracle at Delphi who his parents were. In response, the oracle warned him to avoid his homeland, for it was there he would kill his father and marry his mother. Assuming that Polybus and Merope were really his parents, he resolved never to return to Corinth and took the road from Delphi that led to Thebes. Oedipus tells what happened then in his own words in *Oedipus the King.*

> When I was near the branching of the crossroads,
> going on foot, I was encountered by
> a herald and a carriage with a man in it . . . .
> He that led the way
> and the old man himself wanted to thrust me
> out of the road by force. I became angry
> and struck the coachman who was pushing me.
> When the old man saw this he watched his moment,
> and as I passed he struck me from his carriage,
> full on the head with his two pointed goad.
> But he was paid in full and presently
> my stick had struck him backwards from the car
> and he rolled out of it. And then I killed them
> all.[4]

The old man, whom Oedipus did not recognize, was Laius. The curse of Pelops was being fulfilled.

After the violent encounter at the crossroads, Oedipus came to Thebes, a city that was besieged with troubles. Not only was it now without a king, it was also menaced by the Sphinx ("strangler"), a monster with the head and breasts of a woman, the body of a dog, the tail of a serpent, the wings of a bird, the paws of a lion, and a human voice. The Sphinx asked a riddle of all passers-by. If they could not answer, it killed and ate them. The riddle was: What creature goes sometimes on four legs, sometimes on two, and sometimes on three, and the more legs it has, the weaker it is?

No Theban had been able to answer, and in despair, Creon, the acting ruler and brother to Jocasta, offered the throne and his sister to anyone who could do so. Oedipus solved the riddle. The creature, he said, is a human; as an infant it goes on four legs, in the prime of life upon two, and in old age, with the aid of a stick, on three. Hearing Oedipus' solution, the Sphinx threw itself off the Theban acropolis. Oedipus became the King of Thebes and the husband of the widowed queen, his mother.

Although the twofold prediction (patricide and incest) of the oracle at Delphi had now been fulfilled, Oedipus lived for a number of years in ignorance of the truth. He sired two sons, Polynices and Eteocles, and two daughters, Antigone and Ismene. All seemed well in Thebes, until a pestilence descended. Crops would not grow, cattle became sick in the fields, women could not bear children, people died of unexplained causes. The Thebans learned with dismay from the oracle at Delphi that this pestilence was the result of their keeping Laius' murderer in their midst. Oedipus swore a curse on this killer and vowed to find and punish him.

Oedipus called before him the blind prophet of Apollo, Teiresias, to discover what the old man knew. In the heated interview that occurred, Teiresias said Oedipus himself was the killer of Laius. Oedipus did not believe Teiresias and in a rage dismissed him.

Soon, a messenger brought news from Corinth that Polybus had died and that the people of Corinth wanted Oedipus to become their king. Oedipus was saddened by the news of Polybus' death, but he was also relieved; the possibility of his killing his father no longer existed. He explained to the messenger, however, that he could not return to Corinth while Merope was alive, for the possibility of his marrying his mother still existed. Upon hearing Oedipus' reason for not returning to Corinth, the messenger (the same shepherd who had received Oedipus as an infant from the servant of Laius) revealed that Polybus and Merope were not Oedipus' true parents.

When Oedipus learned that Laius' old servant was still living, he sent for him and forced him to reveal the shattering story of the past. Jocasta, recognizing that her present husband was also her son, hanged herself. Upon seeing her dangling corpse, Oedipus tore the brooches from her robe and blinded himself. Creon again became acting ruler, and Oedipus, at his own request, was banished in accordance with his earlier condemnation of the killer of Laius.

After living for some time in banishment on the outskirts of Thebes, Oedipus, attended by Antigone, moved about from place to place. Much later he came to Colonus in Attica (*Oedipus at Colonus*), where he was accepted by Theseus, the King of Athens.

Ismene joined Oedipus and Antigone and told them of the struggle that had taken place in Thebes between Eteocles and Polynices. The two brothers had agreed to divide the Theban throne between them, ruling in alternate years. But when his year of kingship had elapsed, Eteocles, who ruled first, refused to relinquish the throne and forced Polynices to flee the city.

Polynices appeared unexpectedly at Colonus and pleaded with Oedipus to help him in his cause against Eteocles. But Oedipus, remembering how neither of his sons had come to his aid in the past, vented his anger against them and wished that they might die by each other's hands.

Amid all of the troubles at Thebes, Creon heard of a prophecy that declared the land where Oedipus died and was buried would enjoy peace and prosperity. Thinking to gain these benefits for his own city, Creon went with a band of men to Colonus to bring Oedipus back to Thebes by force. Theseus intervened, however, forcing Creon to surrender Antigone and Ismene, whom he had already captured, and ordering him to depart.

When the time of Oedipus' death drew near, he blessed his daughters, withdrew to a lonely spot, and, in the presence of Theseus alone, spent his final hours. It was rumored that he died peacefully and simply disappeared from the earth.

Although the sufferings of Oedipus were over, the original curse of Pelops haunted the lives of his children (*Antigone*). Antigone had returned with Ismene to Thebes after the death of Oedipus, where Polynices had gathered an army to attack the city in an attempt to overthrow Eteocles. The two brothers killed each other in combat. Creon, now king, honored Eteocles with a state burial, but he left the body of Polynices, whom he regarded as a rebel, to the vultures, forbidding its burial on pain of death.

Outraged by Creon's decree, Antigone resolved to perform the funeral rites for Polynices. She was caught in the act of throwing dirt on the decaying corpse and brought before the infuriated Creon. She justified her act as being in accordance with the overriding laws of the gods. Creon was unrelenting, however, and condemned her to be buried alive in a cave.

Unlike her sister, Ismene had been afraid to defy Creon. She later regretted her lack of courage and came forward to claim a share in Antigone's guilt and punishment, but Creon simply treated Ismene as insane. Creon's son Haemon begged his father to have mercy on Antigone, to whom Haemon was betrothed. When Creon stubbornly refused, Haemon swore that he would die along with her. Only after the prophet Teiresias threatened Creon with the disastrous consequences of his contempt for the divine laws was Creon moved, and he hurried to free Antigone from the cave where she was buried. There he found Haemon embracing the body of his beloved, who had taken her own life by hanging. Before Creon's eyes, Haemon killed himself with a sword. And when Creon returned to the palace, he discovered that Eurydice, his wife, had killed herself as well.

The original curse of Pelops had spelled disaster for three generations within the royal house of Thebes: Laius, Oedipus, and Antigone. With the death of Antigone, the curse was spent.

## Sophocles on What Can I Know?

Sophocles lived in the twilight of the Homeric worldview, according to which life is dominated by blind, mechanical force, which reduces human beings to things and destroys them indiscriminately. In Homer's epics, this force is associated with the whimsy of the gods. "Such is the way the gods spun life for unfortunate mortals," proclaims Achilles, "that we live in unhappiness, but the gods themselves have no sorrows."[5]

At times in Sophocles' plays, the idea of Homeric force appears. To cite examples: in *Antigone*, the messenger says that in human affairs "luck . . . overturns/the happy or unhappy day by day."[6] The chorus in *Antigone*—omniscient observer and interpreter of the action—quote an old saying, "The bad becomes the good to him a god would doom."[7] In *Oedipus at Colonus*, Antigone says, "You will never see in all the world/A man whom God has led/Escape his destiny!"[8] Speeches such as these suggest gods who impose their will without weighing the sufferings of their victims.

For the most part, however, Sophocles' interpretation of the relationship between the gods and humanity differs significantly from that of Homer. Unlike the character Achilles, he doesn't protest against divinity. Rather, he's led by the conviction that, in spite of human suffering, every part of the universe, however ugly or irrational it may appear, fits into the whole and forms a perfect, well-ordered scheme. The gods are keepers of *dike* ("justice"), the principle of order and reason within the universe. Antigone points to this idea of justice when she defends herself before Creon.

> For me it was not Zeus who made that order.
> Nor did that Justice who lives with the gods below
> mark out such laws to hold among mankind.
> Nor did I think your orders were so strong
> that you, a mortal man, could over-run
> the gods' unwritten and unfailing laws.
> Not now, nor yesterday's, they always live
> and no one knows their origin in time.[9]

For Sophocles, it's a matter of intellectual faith that the human being is by nature aware of the justice that pervades the universe. It's the obligation of humans to keep justice in a morally ordered society; failure to do so brings punitive results. When an action reaches beyond the ordinary limits, the universe automatically recoils. This recoil is justice rectifying itself, setting things back in balance.

H. D. F. Kitto explains by means of an analogy how justice functions within the Sophoclean universe. In the realm of physical nature, Kitto observes, too much wetness in the rainy season is followed by too much dryness in the dry season; flood is followed by drought. Thus, nature overcompensates, again causing an imbalance.[10] This analogy helps explain the apparently extravagant retribution the gods impose upon humans who over-step the limits of justice. The gods don't regard the intent of human action so much as its degree of deviation from an existing norm. The universe itself has a principle of moderation built into it, and when humans consciously or unconsciously are excessive, correction, even over-correction, is sure to follow.

A clear indication of justice at work appears in a comment by the chorus as Antigone is being led to the burial cave.

> You went to the furthest verge
> of daring, but there you found
> the high foundation of justice, and fell.
> Perhaps you are paying your father's pain.[11]

Here the chorus intimates that Antigone is paying a price not only for her own action but also for Oedipus', who in turn paid a price for the action of Laius. What makes Antigone's suffering all the more poignant is that she acted out of the deepest of religious convictions. The play doesn't condemn the heroine, but it shows that by acting rightly she violated civil law and thus upset the balance of the social order. Even though the gods favor Antigone, they are concurrently the keepers of justice who must have their due. She goes beyond the acceptable limits, and justice compensates by striking back.

Sophocles' answer, then, to the question What can I know? is an assured one based on a specific concept of justice. He affirms that (1) the laws of the universe are absolute and unyielding; (2) things go on in predetermined ways; and (3) when human action goes too far, correction is immediate and certain.

# Sophocles on What Ought I to Do?

To many a reader, the Sophoclean concept of justice seems unbearably oppressive. If the universe is such that individuals must pay a price not only for their own but also the blunders of others, if the meaning of existence goes on, as it were, over our heads, then what real responsibility can we claim for our own lives? Nowhere do we sense this oppression more strongly than in *Oedipus the King.*

When the play opens, the most important factors—murder and incest—have been established by the past, and the action must take place within their framework. Moreover, an unavoidable course of events must be followed out until the violated divine order has been restored (in Sophocles' account of the Oedipus legend, this happens in *Antigone*). Whether we stress the excessive pride of Oedipus at the beginning of *Oedipus the King* ("I Oedipus whom all men call the Great"[12]) or the innocence of Oedipus, who is ignorant of the terrible deeds he has committed, the objective facts do not change: he is guilty and punishment must ensue.

But in spite of the determinism of the play, another side portrays Oedipus as freely contributing to his own downfall. By pronouncing a curse on the killer, he actually places the curse on himself: "Whoever/he was that killed the king may readily/wish to dispatch me with his murderous hand."[13] And prior to Oedipus' curse, his own cleverness in answering the riddle of the Sphinx put him in a position to marry Jocasta.

In stressing that Oedipus both is and is not responsible for his own downfall, *Oedipus the King* confounds two kinds of thinkers: those on the one hand who insist that a human being has no responsibility whatsoever, and those on the other who insist that a human being's responsibility is total. Sophocles himself defends neither of these specific viewpoints. For him, both are true at once. Oedipus is responsible; his actions are his own. But the pattern of his actions is the same as that predicted by the oracle of Delphi. A main problem of human existence, Sophocles seems to say, is that humans must act on the basis of the knowledge available to them; lacking the total knowledge of the gods, they're bound to make mistakes.

Sophocles never lets us forget that Oedipus makes terrible mistakes in the course of his actions. He is a man who pays an extreme price for knowing more about his own nature. He will not be deterred from knowing who he is, either by the blind prophet, Teiresias, who tells him, "Terrible is wisdom when it brings no profit,"[14] or by his wife, Jocasta, who, having finally recognized the truth herself, says to Oedipus, "God keep you from the knowledge of who you are."[15] Even at the most anguished moment of his existence, Oedipus must have the full story: "I will not be persuaded to let be/the chance of finding out the whole thing clearly."[16] The choice, as Oedipus experiences it, is between living in ignorance and living in truth, between not knowing and knowing, and he finds the prospect of not knowing intolerable. He is Sophocles' emblem of passionate human intelligence, which, for better or worse, presses toward solving all of the riddles.

Are we to assume that in his portrayal of Oedipus, Sophocles is giving us a model for living? Is it incumbent upon us as individuals to pursue knowledge at all costs? Hardly! The weight of meaning in *Oedipus the King* falls on the idea that true knowledge of one's nature goes hand in hand with the recognition of one's essentially subordinate place in the universe. The play insists that the universe is based on a principle of justice that overwhelms any sense of rightness we might hold. The problem of why bad things happen to good or innocent people is simply not reducible to rational formulae.

For Sophocles, there is a tragic element in life, an unbridgeable separation between humanity and divinity, between what the best of human minds can know and what is ultimately knowable. This tragic element calls our schemes of reason and morality into doubt and makes the question What ought I to do? a conundrum. Sophocles was a conservative who believed that the best guidelines for conduct are found in the conventions of tradition. But he was acutely aware that even here, in the case of Oedipus acting to punish a killer or in Antigone acting to bury a brother, acting with assumed propriety can actually contribute to our own ruin, as well as the ruin of others.

## Sophocles on for What Can I Hope?

Sophoclean drama points unceasingly to the tragic element in life, the paradox of a universe whose opposition to humanity can neither be changed nor overlooked. With all of its incongruity and strangeness, its apparent meaninglessness, human existence is a crucible in which courage is tested.

Sophocles does not try to make things easier by offering hope for individual survival beyond the grave. As the old, tattered

Oedipus says in *Oedipus at Colonus*, "The immortal/Gods alone have neither age nor death!/All other things almighty Time disquiets."[17] Sophocles soberly acknowledges the conclusiveness of human existence, whether viewed in its entirety or in the detail of individual destinies. In reading him, we may often find ourselves wondering if he isn't simply an embittered pessimist.

But if we interpret him in this light, how are we to account for those magnificent passages in his work which glorify humanity? Listen to the words he puts into the mouths of the chorus in *Antigone*.

> Many the wonders but nothing walks stranger than man.
> This thing crosses the sea in the winter's storm,
> making his path through the roaring waves.
> And she, the greatest of gods, the earth—
> ageless she is, and unwearied—he wears her away
> as the ploughs go up and down from year to year
> and his mules turn up the soil.
>
> Gay nations of birds he snares and leads,
> wild beast tribes and the salty brood of the sea,
> with the twisted mesh of his nets, this clever man.
> He controls with craft the beasts of the open air,
> walkers on hills. The horse with his shaggy mane
> he holds and harnesses, yoked about the neck,
> and the strong bull of the mountain.
>
> Language, and thought like the wind
> and the feelings that make the town,
> he has taught himself, and shelter against the cold,
> refuge from rain. He can always help himself.
> He faces no future helpless. There's only death
> that he cannot find an escape from.[18]

No, the poet who wrote these words of praise about human accomplishment and possibility is not a pessimist. Sophocles sees a great deal of hope for the human creature. In spite of the tragic element in life, our affairs are often amenable to human resourcefulness. The hardest thing to come to terms with, however, is death.

Sophocles does not lament the human condition, but neither does he blink at its harder truths. Human beings do not create themselves; they discover they've been thrown into the world. In origin and upbringing, every human is affected by circumstances that bear the semblance of fate. No one starts without a history. We cannot change what happened before us; indeed, we have to reckon with the consequences of our predecessors' actions. Furthermore, we direct our actions toward the future and initiate something new, and the results of those actions are outside our strict control; they reverberate beyond us. Everywhere the sovereignty of the human being's will and reason comes into conflict with necessity. The human being is limited and free at the same time, and the crux of human wisdom is to acknowledge this paradox.

By understanding what Sophocles regards as human wisdom, we can appreciate the full measure of Oedipus as a hero in *Oedipus at Colonus*, the last play Sophocles wrote. Oedipus appears chastened ("Suffering and time,/Vast time, have been instructors in contentment"[19]), but not defeated. He realizes what the gods are—severe keepers of justice—but he doesn't blame them for being what they are. He has learned to endure with courage, even dignity, the circumstances of his own life. He knows that the suffering he's experienced far outruns anything he's personally deserved ("No, I did not sin!"[20]). Nonetheless, he reconciles himself with what he could not avoid, and in that lies Oedipus' heroic greatness.

In *Oedipus at Colonus*, Sophocles reminds us that unavoidable suffering, which is the universal human lot, does not have to be futile. It was not futile for Oedipus, for through suffering he achieved a knowledge of his own nature that rivaled even the wisdom of the gods. They who were prescient and immortal did not know what it meant to stumble blindly through life and to face death. Only an Oedipus, a human being, is capable of such knowledge.

After Oedipus dies, the chorus quietly observes, "He lived his life."[21] The whole Sophoclean philosophy of hope is contained in these few words. The hope of humankind, Sophocles declares, resides within the human spirit, whereby we affirm that our endeavors are meaningful in the context in which life is lived. Oedipus ultimately makes this affirmation in spite of everything he experiences as haphazard and against him in the universe.

# Implications of the Sophoclean Image of Human Nature

Life for Sophocles is an untidy, risky business, and he admires that type of human being most who does not resign to fate or circumstance but lives life his or her own way, against the universe. The image of human nature or the ideal of humankind that Sophocles projects is that of a solitary individual who assumes responsibility for his or her own dispositions, responses, and actions in the midst of circumstances over which that individual has no control.

This Sophoclean image of human nature has repeatedly asserted itself in the history of Western thought. It is reflected in such first- and second-century Stoic philosophers as Seneca, Epictetus, and Marcus Aurelius, who assumed that the judicious person acknowledges the limits of his place in an overall scheme of things and strives to fulfill the necessary purposes of that place. The Sophoclean image, in its stoical dimension, seems to have inspired writers such as Michel De Montaigne, in the sixteenth century, and Matthew Arnold, in the nineteenth. In our own century, it's an image that goes hand in hand with the perception of a fragmented world whose motions are at the mercy of blind forces. Joseph Conrad (*Heart of Darkness*), Virginia Woolf (*To the Lighthouse*), Albert Camus (*The Plague*), Ernest Hemingway (*The Old Man and the Sea*), and William Faulkner (*As I Lay Dying*) are moderns who stand within the tradition of the Sophoclean image of human nature. As writers who are drawn to this image, they maintain that life does not make sense, but it's ours to make sense of nonetheless.

Underlying the metaphorical language in which Sophocles expressed himself is an insight that has been captured in that mode of philosophical thought described as *existentialism*. While expressions of this mode of thought vary, perhaps what's common to all existentialists is the notion that an individual life has no essential meaning apart from a courageous act of self-affirmation, whereby one accepts his or her own accidental individuality and assumes responsibility for his or her own actions.

The psychiatrist Victor E. Frankl brings the existential notion of self-affirmation into grim focus in *Man's Search for Meaning*, an account of the author's own struggle for survival in a Nazi concentration camp. Under the harrowing circumstances of life in the camp, Frankl explains, people died every day, either because their deaths were mandated or because they were so crushed by hardship and despair they simply expired. But if one were to survive at all, Frankl notes, a certain attitude had to be adopted.

> What was really needed was a fundamental change in our attitude toward life. We had to learn ourselves and, furthermore, we had to teach the despairing men, that *it did not really matter what we expected from life, but rather what life expected from us.* We needed to stop asking about the meaning of life, and instead to think of ourselves as those who were being questioned by life—daily and hourly. Our answer must consist, not in talk, . . . but in right action and in right conduct.[22]

Frankl maintains that it is "impossible to define the meaning of life in a general way."[23] The question of the meaning of life is always a personal matter; every human must discover, and respond to, what life demands of him or her. No human being and no destiny can be compared with any other human being or any other destiny. "No situation repeats itself, and each situation calls for a different response."[24] For Frankl, the content of our responses imparts to life whatever meaning it might have. He and similar modern thinkers perpetuate the spirit of Sophocles, who gave us in Oedipus a universal image of the human being responding, first with despair, but finally with uncanny resolution, to life's outrageous demands.

# Suggestions for Discussion and Study

1. In *Antigone*, the argument between Antigone and Creon has both a personal and a larger, social dimension. How would you characterize both the personal and the social dimensions of their argument? Compare the claims of the individual as opposed to the claims of the state as they are presented in *Antigone* and Plato's *Apology*, where Socrates defends himself before a large jury of Athenian citizens. Both Antigone and

Socrates are forced to choose between defiance and loss of their individuality. Both die for their causes. In the lives of what individuals today do we see the dilemma that Antigone and Socrates faced?

2. Notice the character of Ismene in both *Oedipus at Colonus* and *Antigone.* She appears to be weaker than Antigone in both plays, yet when she does show strength by choosing to share Antigone's guilt and punishment, Antigone rejects her. Speculate on Antigone's motives for rejecting her and whether or not these motives are upstanding.

3. How has Creon's role and character changed from *Oedipus the King* to *Oedipus at Colonus*? In Creon's transformation, is Sophocles pointing to the temptations and dangers that go with the wielding of power?

4. How has Oedipus' character changed from *Oedipus the King* to *Oedipus at Colonus*? Toward the conclusion of the latter play, Oedipus regains something of his former self. In spite of the loss of his kingship, he is imperial in his attitude toward Polynices, and he goes to his grave giving orders to King Theseus about how he wishes to be buried. What idea, if any, is Sophocles trying to reinforce about Oedipus' character as he approaches death?

5. Explore all the motives for Oedipus' insistence that the place of his burial be kept secret.

6. At the heart of Sophocles' outlook upon life is an attitude of accepting the inevitable. This attitude runs counter to the modern temper, perhaps best symbolized in Zarathustra, Nietzsche's creature of will who aspires to be the sovereign shaper and controller of his own destiny. With Sophocles' Oedipus on the one side, and Nietzsche's Zarathustra on the other, we have a classic and a romantic outlook upon life. Toward which outlook are you inclined? Are the two outlooks reconcilable? (The possibility of such reconciliation is explored in Robert M. Pirsig's *Zen and the Art of Motorcycle Maintenance*.)

7. One of the most celebrated comments in modern times on *Oedipus the King* comes from Sigmund Freud, who wrote:

The *Oedipus Rex* is a tragedy of fate: its tragic effect depends on the conflict between the all-powerful will of the gods and the vain efforts of human beings threatened with disaster; resignation to the divine will, and the perception of one's own impotence is the lesson which the deeply moved spectator is supposed to learn from the tragedy. Modern authors have therefore sought to achieve a similar tragic effect by expressing the same conflict in stories of their own invention. But the playgoers have looked on unmoved . . . ; the modern tragedies of destiny have failed of their effect.

If the *Oedipus Rex* is capable of moving a modern reader or playgoer no less powerfully than it moved the contemporary Greeks, the only possible explanation is that the effect of the Greek tragedy does not depend upon the conflict between fate and human will, but upon the peculiar nature of the material by which this conflict is revealed. There must be a voice within us which is prepared to acknowledge the compelling power of fate in the *Oedipus* . . . . His fate moves us only because it might have been our own, because the oracle laid upon us before our birth the very curse which rested upon him. It may be that we were all destined to direct our first sexual impulses toward our mothers and our first impulses of hatred and violence toward our fathers; our dreams convince us that we were. ("The Interpretation of Dreams," in *The Basic Writings of Sigmund Freud*, trans. and ed. A. A. Brill [New York: Random House, The Modern Library, 1938], pp. 307–308).

Freud's Oedipus complex theory has been much discussed and often disputed. Is it true that we are destined to direct our first sexual impulses toward our opposite-sex parent and our first impulses of hatred toward the other? Nevertheless, the Freudian interpretation of *Oedipus the King* prompts us to consider that the modern human being labors as much under the concept of *fate* as did Sophocles. To what extent does this concept come into play when we contemplate such issues as genetics, race, nationalism, social class, economics?

# Further Reading

Bowra, C. M. *Sophoclean Tragedy*. London: Oxford University Press, 1970. An interpretation of each of Sophocles' seven plays and an attempt to say what Sophoclean tragedy is.

Kitto, H. D. F. *Greek Tragedy: A Literary Study*. London: Methuen & Co. Ltd., 1966. A highly authoritative study of Sophocles and the whole of Greek tragedy.

Knox, Bernard M. W. *The Heroic Temper: Studies in Sophoclean Tragedy.* Berkeley: University of California Press, 1964. Seeks to explore the Sophoclean vision of the hero in both its general characteristics and specific manifestations.

Waldock, A. J. A. *Sophocles the Dramatist.* Cambridge: At the University Press, 1966. Approaches Sophocles as a dramatist rather than as a poet or an exponent of ideas.

Whitman, Cedric H. *Sophocles: A Study of Heroic Humanism.* Cambridge, MA: Harvard University Press, 1951. Discusses Sophocles against the mythological and philosophical background in which he wrote.

# Notes

1. Karl Jaspers, *The Origin and Goal of History* (New Haven, CT: Yale University Press, 1965), p. 1.
2. Plato, *Apology*, in *Plato: The Collected Dialogues*, eds. Edith Hamilton and Huntington Cairns (Princeton, NJ: Princeton University Press, 1973), 38a.
3. Werner Jaeger, *Paideia: The Ideal of Greek Culture*, 2 vols., trans. Gilbert Highet (New York: Oxford University Press, 1945), I: 271.
4. Sophocles, *Oedipus the King*, in *Sophocles I: Oedipus the King, Oedipus at Colonus, Antigone*, trans. David Grene, Robert Fitzgerald, Elizabeth Wyckoff (Chicago: The University of Chicago Press, 1954), lines 801–813. (All quotations from Sophocles' plays are from this edition, hereafter cited only by title and line numbers.)
5. Homer, *The Iliad of Homer*, trans. Richmond Lattimore (Chicago: The University of Chicago Press, 1951), bk. 24, lines 525–526.
6. *Antigone*, op. cit., lines 1158–1159.
7. Ibid., lines 621–622.
8. *Oedipus at Colonus*, op. cit., lines 251–253.
9. *Antigone*, op. cit., lines 450–457.
10. H. D. F. Kitto, *Greek Tragedy: A Literary Study* (London: Methuen & Co. Ltd., 1973), p. 135.
11. *Antigone*, op. cit., lines 852–855.
12. *Oedipus the King*, op. cit., line 8.
13. Ibid., lines 138–140.
14. Ibid., lines 316–317.
15. Ibid., line 1068.
16. Ibid., lines 1065–1066.
17. *Oedipus at Colonus*, op. cit., lines 607–609.
18. *Antigone*, op. cit., lines 331–360.
19. *Oedipus at Colonus*, op. cit., lines 6–7.
20. Ibid., line 538.
21. Ibid., line 1702.

22. Victor E. Frankl, *Man's Search for Meaning* (New York: Simon & Schuster, Pocket Books, 1963), p. 122.
23. Ibid.
24. Ibid., p. 123.

# ·3·

# AUGUSTINE
## and the image of
# FAITH

# Cultural Background

Eight centuries elapsed between the time of Sophocles and Augustine. During those centuries, the Western and Near Eastern world changed its political character several times: Philip of Macedon brought Greece under his power; his son, Alexander the Great, conquered Persia and eventually the whole of the ancient world as far south as Egypt and as far east as India; Julius Caesar solidified the Roman Republic under his authority and pushed the influence of Rome northward from the Mediterranean into the heartland of western Europe; his grandnephew Octavian, or Augustus, completed the transformation of the Roman state from Republic to Empire; and Christianity, which was destined to become a powerful political force, made its appearance in the world under the reign of Augustus and was endorsed as an official religion of the Empire under the rule of Constantine.

Aurelius Augustine lived at a time when classical culture, as expressed in the Roman world, was in danger of being destroyed. The frontiers of the Empire in the west were yielding to the northern hordes who already had Gaul and Spain in their hands and were menacing Italy. As a thinker, Augustine was largely responsible for pulling together the enduring elements of the classical view of life and fusing them with a Christian view. In him, two great traditions in Western thought came together: the Greco-Roman literary and philosophic tradition and the Judeo-Christian biblical tradition. Plato, Plotinus, and Cicero chiefly influenced Augustine from the Greco-Roman side, the writers of Genesis and St. Paul on the biblical side.

We see Augustine at the furthest reach of his powers in *The City of God*, a book that was thirteen years in the writing. In this work, he assumed a number of roles: theologian, apologist, philosopher, moralist, political thinker, literary critic, and interpreter of history. In its intellectual scope and depth, *The City of God* warrants comparison with Plato's *The Republic*.

The central concept of *The Republic* is the question of humanity's right life, or justice, which is at the same time the question of the right order of society. If the rivaling elements of an individual's soul—appetite, spirit, and reason—are rightly ordered and arranged, he or she is just. Consequently, that individual will also act justly in relation with others, by staying in his or her own station, by living the kind of life he or she was meant to live.

Augustine transformed Plato's secular concept of justice into a religious one: the essence of justice is the relation between humanity and God, from which right relations between individuals will inevitably follow. But in spite of this revision, Augustine maintained, like Plato, that the idea and similitude of justice is the same for the individual as it is for collective society. For both of these thinkers, society was human nature written large; insofar as individuals attained the perfection of their nature, so they would attain the perfection of society.

Plato assumed that to answer the important questions facing humankind—how to live, how to organize society, and all questions of value—demanded not only information but also considerable skill in abstract reasoning. Augustine appreciated Platonic high-mindedness (the insistence on abstract reasoning), but he maintained that the perfection of human nature is the work of divine providence. Here we see the biblical, especially Pauline, influence on Augustine's thought. And, since for Augustine the events of history manifested the workings of providence, the Christian point of view preoccupied not only his revision of the Platonic view of human nature but also of the entire classical view of life.

## Biography

Augustine's autobiography, *The Confessions*, narrates his life from childhood to middle age. He was born in A.D. 354 in Tagaste, an agricultural village in northern Africa that is Souk Ahras in modern Algeria, near the border of Tunisia. His mother, Monica, was a Christian; his father, Patricius, a pagan. Under his mother's influence he was guided in Christian teachings, but in accordance with the custom of the time, he was not baptized as a child.

Although Augustine's parents were poor, they gave him the best education they could afford, first in Tagaste, and then in nearby Madaura. In these schools, he received a solid grounding in grammar and Latin literature. When Augustine was sixteen years old, his father died. The boy's formal education might have ended at this time had it not been for a wealthy businessman,

Romanianus, who became his benefactor and made it possible for him to go to Carthage. Here, in 370, he studied rhetoric, a subject that was to prepare the student for a career in the courts of law.

A few months after arriving in Carthage, a cultural melting pot of the ancient world, Augustine began living with a concubine, who in 372 gave birth to a son. (Years later, in writing *The Confessions*, he looked back upon this segment of his life with mixed emotions. He had deep affection for the son, Adeodatus [who died at age seventeen or eighteen], but he regretted that he had brought upon himself and others, through wayward passion, the trials that ensued from the whole affair.) Thus, in his late teens Augustine found himself the head of a family. The three moved to Tagaste where, as a means of earning a living, Augustine opened a small school and taught rhetoric for a year. The following year, they moved back to Carthage, where Augustine again opened a school and continued to teach.

A chief advantage of Augustine's profession was that it gave him the opportunity to read widely and to develop his own thought. He found his taste for philosophy quickened, first by reading Cicero's praise of the pursuit of wisdom, in the *Hortensius* (now lost), and then by reading a translation of Aristotle's *On the Categories*. But by far the most important influence on him during his years at Carthage was his study and practice of Manicheanism.

Born in Persia, Mani (216–277), the founder of Manicheanism, absorbed Persian and Babylonian thought and combined it with what he understood of Christianity. Accordingly, he taught that universal matter—the physical universe, or nature—is governed by two principles: light, or good, and darkness, or evil, which are in constant strife with one another.

The Manicheans' view of human nature affirmed that in each individual there are two souls, or forces: one good and one bad, one light and one dark. These two forces steadily exert pressure upon the conduct of the individual; what he or she does is the result of these two opposing forces. It is a mechanical view of human conduct. The human being participates in the strife that goes on between light and darkness, and in that strife the human being can perform only by resisting action that would result in the further entanglement of light with darkness. To this end the Manicheans prescribed all kinds of ascetic practices (which they did not universally adhere to), such as abstinence from sexual relations and the refusal to kill animals or to eat meat.

What appealed to Augustine in Manicheanism seems to have been (1) its claim to an intellectual understanding of the universe and human nature, and (2) its moral code, which spoke directly to his own sensual nature and the anxieties it had caused him. As an adherent of Manicheanism, he found a system of thought whereby he could fulfill his intellectual demands—to know the essence of things—and resolve his personal moral struggles. After nearly a decade of association with the Manichees, however, he expressed his disappointment with both the intellectual and moral aspects of Manichean teachings.

Augustine became increasingly disenchanted with life in Carthage. His students were unruly, and he was eager to make a name for himself in more sophisticated intellectual circles. Thus, he went to Rome in 383, leaving his concubine and son behind in Carthage. After only a year in Rome (teaching students who were relatively well-behaved but who failed to pay their tuitions), he obtained from the prefect Symmachus a government appointment to teach rhetoric in Milan—then the western capital of the Roman Empire.

Augustine's years in Milan were momentous. He had disavowed Manicheanism, and for a time was attracted to the skeptical philosophy of the Academics, who held that it was impossible to know anything with absolute certitude and that the prudent person would withhold judgment on speculative questions, attending to the practical affairs of everyday living. But this preoccupation with skepticism did not last long. Augustine began reading Neoplatonic writings and attending the sermons of Ambrose, Bishop of Milan—a combination of influences that prepared the way for his conversion.

The exact sources of Augustine's familiarity with Neoplatonism are unknown. The *Enneads* of Plotinus had been recently translated from Greek into Latin, and the works of other teachers whom Augustine usually referred to merely as *The Platonists* were available, though the dialogues of Plato himself probably were not. The system of thought Augustine discovered in Neoplatonism was quite different from the one he had discovered in Manicheanism. Humans commit evil, the Neoplatonists taught, not because they are the victims of the opposing forces of light and dark, but because they lack a knowledge of the Good. Humans can control their base emotions and their irrational nature and thereby develop morally and spiritually.

It would seem, however, that Bishop Ambrose had an even more immediate impact on Augustine than his study of Neoplatonists. Through this powerful, eloquent churchman, Augustine became acquainted with a different version of Christianity than any he had previously known. His mother had taught him Bible stories when he was a boy, and her influence had followed him through the intervening years of his career. But Ambrose showed him, by allegorical interpretation, how to understand Scripture in such a fashion that it no longer seemed naive to his highly trained intellect. Ambrose had the kind of personal certainty and security that Augustine desired and so far lacked.

When he was thirty-two years old, Augustine converted to Christianity in the dramatic manner he recounts in *The Confessions*. While seated in a garden in Milan, he heard a child's voice chanting over and over the words *Tolle lege* ("Take up and read"[1]). Were these the words of a child's game or divine instruction? Augustine took up a Bible and read the first passage on which his eyes fell, Romans 13:13, 14. "Not in rioting and drunkenness, not in chambering and wantonness, not in strife and envying. But put ye on the Lord Jesus Christ, and make not provision for the flesh, to *fulfil* the lusts" (KJV). This experience in the garden convinced Augustine that in Christianity he had found the true meaning and way of life. A year later at Easter, he was baptized by Bishop Ambrose.

After his baptism, Augustine decided to return to Africa, but the death of his mother (who had followed him to Milan) at Rome's seaport, Ostia, delayed the journey for several months. The year 388, nonetheless, found him back in Tagaste, where he founded a small religious community with friends. In 391 he was ordained a priest; and five years later, when Valerius, the Bishop of Hippo, died, Augustine was chosen to fill his place. The teacher and philosopher who had become a theologian now became the pastor of his flock. As Bishop of Hippo, Augustine assumed a weight of administrative duties, all the while writing a dialogue with various dissenting factions of the church. The bulk of his voluminous writings defended Christianity as he had come to experience and interpret it. He died in 430, in the last days of Roman political certainty in the West. At the very moment of his death, the Vandals were at the gates of Hippo.

# Augustine on What Can I Know?

Nowhere in Augustine's writings is his theory of knowledge presented in a systematic fashion; rather, he expresses it incidentally in the course of exploring various other subjects. The theory that he does express owes a great deal to the Platonic doctrine of ideas, which he absorbed through his study of Neoplatonic thinkers. What is this Platonic doctrine, and to what extent is it manifested in the thought of Augustine?

When Plato spoke of ideas he often meant what we would recognize as concepts, such as the concept of a circle. But he also spoke of the idea of ideas. Let's briefly illustrate. When we define the circle as the locus of all points equidistant from the center, this concept is valid for all circles. We may say the concept presides over everything big or small, near or far that has circularity. But for Plato, the mind is never satisfied as long as it must still ask for a fuller explanation of things, and the fuller explanation we may ask of circularity is why there should be such an idea in the first place. Plato's ultimate question was, What is the idea which presides over all ideas? He called this unitary idea of ideas *the Good*.

Plato uses such a moralistic term for his last word on knowledge because, as he tells us in the *Phaedo*,[2] his Good connotes obligation, or *ought*. All ideas ought to make sense, which means that they inherently do make sense to anyone capable of grasping their meaning. The burden of making sense is not on ideas but on the human mind. Ideas themselves are simply what they *are*, and as such they are the mind's proper objects.

For Plato, it's impossible to define the idea of ideas. What is definable is always a specific idea that comes *under* the idea of ideas. The latter presides over all inquiry and over all truth. Plato offers an analogy, which explains that the Good in the realm of thought is like the sun in the realm of the visible. We do not see the sun, but we see everything in its light. What the sun is to the eye and to what is seen, the Good is to reason (the human being's highest faculty) and thought. If the mind is constantly directed toward that which is illumined by the light of the Good, it seems to possess reason and it knows.[3] Whatever obscurities may attend the Platonic doctrine of ideas for us as moderns, it's clear Plato envisioned the Good as the inescapable, live challenge, the ground of possibility of all thought and truth.

Augustine found the Platonic vision of the Good, as mediated through Neoplatonism, to be compatible with his own interpretation of human nature. Of course, as a Christian, Augustine spoke of the quest for God where Plato spoke of the quest for the Good. But Augustine's quest, like Plato's, was governed by the conviction that things ought to make sense, and we ought to look for it. Augustine makes his position on this matter clear in his treatise *Against the Skeptics*, where he argues that if things did not make sense, we could not think at all; that is, we could never look for any meaning. Our mind is a reasoning mind, and if we look for the ground of possibility of reason, we'll find it lies in the idea of truth. If truth were only a word, only human opinion, as the Academics claimed, then all argumentation would be a meaningless mental activity without a real orientation.

So far, it may sound as though Augustine simply adopted the Platonic theory of knowledge uncritically, without adding anything of his own. In developing his own theory, however, he did add something distinctive. Having acknowledged with Plato that we are rational creatures who live under the authority of the idea of truth, Augustine went on to differ about where the truth is to be found. It's not to be found, he insisted, in a timeless region beyond the constellations, as Platonic language implied. It's to be found within our own individual nature, within the self. In his treatise *Of True Religion*, Augustine writes:

> Do not go abroad. Return within yourself. In the inward man dwells truth. If you find that you are by nature mutable, transcend yourself. But remember in doing so that you must also transcend yourself even as a reasoning soul. Make for the place where the light of reason is kindled. What does every good reasoner attain but truth? And yet truth is not reached by reasoning, but is itself the goal of all who reason. There is an agreeableness than which there can be no greater. Agree, then, with it. Confess

> that you are not as it is. It has to do no seeking, but you reach it by seeking, not in space, but by a disposition of mind, so that the inward man may agree with the indwelling truth in a pleasure that is . . . supremely spiritual.[4]

In attempting to come to grips with this passage, and the theory of knowledge it embodies, we need to remind ourselves that Augustine is speaking not only philosophically but also religiously. In a dialogue with his son titled *The Teacher*, Augustine says that to gain knowledge "we do not listen to anyone speaking and making sounds outside ourselves. We listen to Truth which presides over our minds within us, though of course we may be bidden to listen by someone using words."[5] Augustine calls this inner teacher "Christ." Behind this view is the belief that we cannot think at all without recourse to knowledge, gained from God, of ourselves and the world. When Augustine says we find truth within ourselves, it's in recognition that the truth of the mind's ideas is grounded in God, who is the Creator of mind and its objects and who illuminates the mind to equip it to know.

Here's where the whole issue of *faith* (giving assent to those things we do not yet fully understand) enters into Augustine's theory of knowledge. He was much attracted to the text of Isaiah 7:9 in the Septuagint (a Greek translation of the Old Testament): *nisi credideritis, non intelligetis* ("unless you will have believed, you will not understand"). Through Augustine, as Etienne Gilson indicates, this text inspired the discussions of the relationship between faith and reason that persisted throughout medieval intellectualism, giving rise to the formulaic expression, *faith seeking understanding*.[6] How does Augustine see the relationship between faith and understanding?

In *Eighty-Three Different Questions*, Augustine explains that three classes of things are objects of belief. First, there are things that are always believed but never understood: these are events in human history that are not witnessed by the believer. Second, there are other things that are understood as soon as they are believed: these are items such as mathematical solutions and truths in the various sciences. Third, there are things that must first be believed and then later understood.

It's clear that the notion of faith seeking understanding applies particularly to the third, special class concerned with "divine things," or ultimate truths about God. Unlike the first class, but like the second, these truths can be understood, for they are grounded in the mind of God, who makes them known to the knower. Unlike the second class, however, knowledge of these truths is not simultaneous with believing them. Rather, this knowledge comes only to those who first believe in God so that they attain the necessary condition of mind to understand these truths.[7]

All of this may strike us as complex, but there's a simple, practical insight to be gained from Augustine's deliberations. Underlying them is the assumption that any mental act of assent is an act of faith, provided it's not based on unarguable truth, such as the truism that human beings ordinarily walk on two legs.

From the Augustinian standpoint, the intention to be rational in the pursuit of knowledge does not operate autonomously. We don't receive the phenomena of the world entirely free from preconceptions or expectations about what we'll find there or how we'll understand the data that we observe. These expectations form the guidelines of our thought by which we interpret our experience, and rather than exhibiting the self-evidently rational character of the world itself, they are the implicit patterns by which we think.

Why is it, Augustine asks in *The Confessions*, that one person merely stares at the world while another both looks and questions? Why does the world appear one way to this person, another to that? If it does appear the same to both persons, why is it silent to one and yet speaks to the other? He concludes that the world actually "speaks to all, but only those understand who compare its voice taken in from outside with the truth within them."[8]

Here is the center of Augustine's theory of knowledge, which may be expressed in varied but related ways: (1) knowledge depends on hunches; (2) we seek to understand what we have already found through insight: (3) knowledge is presupposed in the initial act of believing; and (4) we shape life in accordance with the content of our affections. A modern American poet captures the sense of the Augustinian theory of knowledge when he writes, "I learn by going where I have to go."[9] From the Augustinian perspective, we may interpret faith seeking understanding to mean that our expectations determine the direction in which we'll look for truth or explanations; they provide the usually unstated but controlling conditions that explanations must meet if they are to be satisfactory. Reason does not precede faith; faith precedes reason.

# Augustine on What Ought I to Do?

The quest for truth starts with faith in God and proceeds in the context of a morally ordered life. Every philosophical and theological notion that Augustine developed was directed in one way or another at the problem of the moral life. For him, everything culminates in clarifying the road to happiness, which is a goal that cannot be separated from questions of human conduct. To get a complete picture of Augustine's moral theory, then, we'd have to comment on virtually all that he wrote. Here we will concentrate on three ideas within Augustine's work that are indispensable to his moral theory: the nature of evil, the nature of the will, and the nature of love.

## The Nature of Evil

In the dialogue *On Free Will*, which Augustine wrote in reaction to the Manichees during the first years after his conversion to Christianity, he reached an interpretation of evil from which he never, in principle, later deviated. What attracted him to Manicheanism in the first place was its claim to an intellectual understanding of the physical universe and human nature. But once he became acquainted with Neoplatonism, Manicheanism appeared to him to be so erroneous that it had to be refuted.

The main way in which it was erroneous was in presupposing an evil principle in the very existence of the physical universe; the evil human beings commit, they commit by reason of an essentially natural operation upon them. Manicheanism had the undesirable effect (at least to Augustine the Christian convert) of establishing two gods or forces, one good and one bad, and of making the moral life of the individual a battleground in the struggle that went on constantly between these two forces.

Augustine found in Neoplatonic thinkers an explanation of evil that was greatly superior to the Manichean, namely, that God has created the universe, and everything in it is good. In nature itself there is nothing evil or bad. Even pestilent insects, poisonous snakes, and beasts of prey have their proper place in the natural order. They contribute to an intricate totality that is as God willed it to be. The Neoplatonic philosophy taught Augustine to think about evil as a lapse in creation rather than as something that asserts itself.

Let's illustrate this kind of Neoplatonic thinking as it would apply to human conduct. When we want to denote something wayward or evil in human conduct, we sometimes revert to animal imagery. If a person who is capable of self-control, as an animal is not, behaves cruelly in relation to others, we may refer to that person as, say, a wolf. The evil consists not in wolfishness, which in the natural order of things is neutral, but in the decline of a person to a status that is subhuman. It is the loss of one's proper place in the order of nature, the "not occupying" that place, that signifies evil. Only human beings, creatures who are gifted with imagination and rational choice, have the capacity for this kind of reversal. The unreasoning animals cannot be said to be capable of evil, because they are limited to the places in the natural order intended for them by the Creator.

### The Nature of the Will

The view that moral evil is a lapse in creation involves Augustine in an exploration of the nature of the will. In following him on this subject, we notice how his treatment represents a significant shift from the classical tradition of philosophy. In *Protagoras*,[10] Plato reports that Socrates said nobody does evil or wrong willingly. What Plato implies by this claim is that there is confusion at the center of evildoers' thinking. If they really know what they're doing, they cannot choose to do it. Plato thought of the will as an automatic corollary of reason. Reason is by definition that which is intent upon the good. To know the good is to do it.

But Augustine rejects the Platonic notion that reason in itself can do no wrong. Contrary to what Plato had assumed about morality, it's not the sub-rational parts of our make-up that are the source of confusion and wrongdoing. Augustine maintains that it's not our appetites and emotional drives that cause us to choose; they only lead us in this or that direction. In the final analysis, it's our rational will that chooses; the choice of evil is the act of reason itself.

Augustine at this point is far less optimistic about human nature than Plato. If for Plato evil is essentially the result of *ignorance*, for Augustine it is essentially the result of pride, the term in his vocabulary that points to a certain perverse element at the core of human nature. A human being may know the good, even what is good *for* him or her, and still not choose it.

*The Confessions* contains several examples of pride at work in Augustine's own life, but none is more representative than his account of stealing pears as a child.

> In a garden nearby to our vineyard there was a pear tree, loaded with fruit that was desirable neither in appearance nor in taste. Late one night—to which hour, according to our pestilential custom, we had kept up our street games— a group of very bad youngsters set out to shake down and rob this tree. We took great loads of fruit from it, not for our own eating, but rather to throw it to the pigs.[11]

Why did the "bad youngsters" commit such malicious acts? Why should a person steal, be wasteful, deliberately contradict what he or she knows is right? Augustine asks himself these same questions: "For I stole a thing of which I had plenty of my own and of much better quality. Nor did I wish to enjoy that thing which I desired to gain by theft."[12] Augustine sees his childhood escapade of stealing pears as symbolizing the pride that universally besets human beings. But when it comes to explaining why such pride should exist, he recognizes the limits of speculation. In the dialogue *On Free Will*, when he anticipates that Evodius is about to ask him why humans choose not to choose the good, Augustine averts the question by saying, "I do not know."[13]

## The Nature of Love

What Augustine does know, and comes emphatically to insist upon in his later years, is that morality, including that which is contained in the Platonic tradition of the virtues, is subsumed in Christianity under the rubric of love. One of his most famous expressions is, "Love, and do what you will,"[14] which means that where love is, no other morality is necessary. But like many pithy expressions by great thinkers, this one, lifted out of context, is subject to misinterpretation. Let's recreate the requisite context in which it can be understood.

Augustine conceives of love in terms of longing, or *desire*. Our whole life, he assumes, is exhausted in seeking one thing or another, and behind all of this seeking is the quest for a condition of ultimate well-being, or happiness. If we aspire to bodily pleasures, friendship, material goods, fame, these are merely means to the end. They are satisfying only to the extent that they allow us to participate in the happiness we seek.

Every person, according to Augustine, is involved in dynamic relationships with objects of desire. Within these relationships, love is not independent and supreme over against its objects. Objects have an attraction of their own that evokes our love and causes us to pursue them as holding the promise of happiness.[15] Indeed, we would not pursue any object unless we imagined it held this promise. It's quite possible, however, to be mistaken in our imagining. When Augustine says, "Love, and do what you will," he's not condoning just any object of love. The desire for some objects leads to misery and discord. He's specific on this subject: "Crime, adultery, villainy, murder, excesses of all kinds, are they not the work of love?"[16] What's incumbent on us morally is that we "cleanse" our love: "turn into the garden the water that was running down the drain."[17]

Only one object can satisfy our quest for happiness, and that is God. Only the divine life can satisfy because it is the ultimate principle of the universe. Human desire, though finite in its manifestations, is infinite in its aspirations. God is the infinite and creative ground of all that is, Augustine holds, and therefore the only right, complete correlative of human desire. In reflecting on the right object of desire, Augustine's principal appeal is not to philosophical reason but to religious inspiration and intuition. What finally emerges in his thought in regard to moral theory is a vigorous theocentrism. Against this background we must understand his expression, "Love, and do what you will." Love of God, which is the highest impulse of human conduct, generates whatever moral rules are necessary. Under the sway of this love, doing what one "will" is identical with doing the good.

In following Augustine as a thinker, we sometimes feel we must stand on tiptoe to get a glimpse of the ideas he's surveying.

But the center of his theory of morality is clear: the pattern of human conduct is decided by the kind of thing(s) a person loves. Nothing makes conduct good or bad except good or bad loves. How important love is to Augustine, and how he makes it his standard of judgment, is reflected in the following passage:

> There are . . . two loves, of which one is holy, the other unclean; one turned towards the neighbor, the other centered on self; one looking to the common good . . . , the other bringing the common good under its own power, arrogantly looking to domination; one subject to God, the other rivaling Him; one tranquil, the other tempestuous; one peaceful, the other seditious; one preferring truth to false praise, the other eager for praise of any sort; one friendly, the other envious; one wishing for its neighbor what it wishes for itself, the other seeking to subject its neighbor to itself; one looking for its neighbor's advantage in ruling its neighbor, the other looking for its own advantage.[18]

These are the words of a thinker who is steeped in biblical tradition. In answer to the question What ought I to do? Augustine would say, Practice "holy" love, for in that the whole of moral obligation lies.

## Augustine on for What Can I Hope?

Augustine sees love of God as the basic principle of morality, but not of *salvation*, which can be brought about only by God. Here we are on the threshold of discussing Augustine's idea of *providence*, his belief in a divinity who guides, governs, and guards the whole course of the universe. This central Augustinian motif rejects any notion that humankind is in control of its own destiny. To see how Augustine develops the idea of providence, we can confidently take as our guide Charles Norris Cochrane's *Christianity and Classical Culture,* a book that amply defines the worldview espoused in Augustine's *City of God.*

Augustine was prompted to write *The City of God* during the pillage of Rome by Alaric and the Goths in 410. The forces of disorder broke in to the Empire, and the very basis of culture was undermined. Alarmed at these events, the Romans were looking for something to blame; the most immediate object was the Christian church. Here was an institution that, up to a century earlier, had been persecuted by the Roman government, but by gradual means it had successfully gained power, prestige, property, and, finally, imperial favor. In the opinion of non-Christian Romans, the gods were angry, and the pillage of Rome was a sign of their anger. As a polemicist and bishop of the church, Augustine answered these pagan attacks on Christianity.

He pointed out that this was not the first time misfortune had come upon the Roman people. Long before Christianity appeared, droughts, famine, military reversals, and misfortunes of various kinds had come again and again. People simply had been lulled into a false sense of security by the long period of Roman domination throughout the world. Augustine went on to assert, however, that the old order of society was facing destruction, primarily because of a deep-seated split in the whole order of existence, or the two essential kinds of human community: those who are intent upon God, and those who are intent upon themselves.

To describe these two kinds of communities, Augustine appropriates the terms the *city of God* and the *earthly city*. The term *civitas* ("city") had been used in various ways by classical thinkers, usually denoting a political or social community. Cicero had specified that one might properly talk of a city where justice—or harmony between the good of the individual and the good of the community—is enforced as the pattern of social behavior.[19] Augustine assumes that if justice were the principle required for a community to exist, it would be impossible to find any community on earth. He agrees in principle that justice ought to exist, but he's convinced that it's never been adequately realized because of human fallibility.

Augustine suggests that what we should mean by the term community is a substantial number of people bound together by common interest. Interest, in this sense, is another way of referring to the Augustinian concept of love. That which a person loves determines the direction of his or her conduct; this is true whether we are speaking of an individual or a group. Interest, or love, can turn in only two directions. If turned toward knowledge of and service to God (or service to other humans as creatures of God), it is love of the city of God. If turned toward satisfaction of self—creaturely pleasures and the drive for personal power—it is love of the earthly city.

In *The City of God*, Augustine speaks with the great weight of biblical narrative, from Genesis to Revelation, behind him. Even before the beginning of human life, in the angelic order that preceded the creation of Adam and Eve, the two opposing communities existed. The fallen angels were the heavenly counterpart of fallen human beings, and once the earthly drama began, the two cities developed side by side. Among Adam's sons, Cain was the founder of the earthly city, while Abel and Seth carried on the line that led into an expanding city of God.[20]

The whole of the Old Testament is the story of parallel great political empires, the prototypes being Assyria in the old days of the East and Rome in the newer West. These two empires are merely the chief instances of a long series of such communities intent primarily upon gaining, maintaining, and increasing their own power. This is political authority without any concern for justice; it is, in effect, banditry or piracy on a large scale.[21]

Augustine insists that political government as such is not bad; indeed, government is necessary for keeping the perversions of human nature in check. But when rulers, in whose hands government is centered, use their power for self-aggrandizement rather than for the common good, political sovereignty becomes a tool in the service of evil. This sort of distortion dominates great empires. In the previous stages of human history, the earthly city has had the upper hand, reducing the community of servants of God to an oppressed minority. Nevertheless, the city of God has proven indestructible. All efforts to crush it have resulted, instead, in its further propagation, and therein the work of providence has been discernible.[22]

With the coming of Christ, Augustine insists, the city of God assumes a new character, to be specified not merely in terms of a general allegiance to God (exemplified even by the pagan philosophers, especially the Platonists, in their seeking of the Good), but in terms of the Christian church. The church is the earthly manifestation, visible and growing, of that community of servants who have been known to God before all ages and who are beginning at last to emerge into a recognizable social institution. The church as such, however, is not the city of God; it contains both those who belong to that city, as well as those who belong to the earthly city. The same pew may hold both saint and sinner; the sorting out of the true servants from the untrue servants will come in that future age when history reaches its divinely appointed consummation.[23]

This consummation will be accompanied by the glorification to supreme happiness of the true servants. The idea of *predestination*—the notion that even before the foundations of the world God destined certain persons for glory—is an idea Augustine developed in treatises such as *Enchiridion* and *On the Gift of Perseverance*. It is an area of his thought that many interpreters have found troubling. Hannah Arendt calls it "the most dubious and also most terrible of his teachings."[24] Be that as it may, it is inherent to Augustine's vision of a divinity on whom all things are dependent.

In discussing the end time of history, Augustine employs highly picturesque language. The divine judgment will involve the final separation of the two communities. As their primary punishment, those who are members of the condemned earthly city will suffer eternal separation from God, and therefore the eternal insatiable craving that only association with God can satisfy. Augustine represents this torment in terms of perpetually burning flames. This is the second death: not the death of the body that we'll all endure, but the death of the spirit, the source of personal potential and fulfillment. It is not annihilation, for annihilation would not be punishment. In the inexorable judgment of God, those who have been intent upon themselves will continuously experience the consequences of that corruption, while those who belong to the city of God will pass into eternal life in which the chief beatitude is the vision of God. Their whole range of powers and possibilities will be fulfilled.

In their final state, inhabitants of the city of God will be beautiful and perfect, with the physical bodies of comely men and women. If one among the baptized dies in infancy, he or she will appear in heaven as a mature person. If one dies in old age, on the other hand, he or she will be restored to vigorous young maturity.[25] So the heavenly city of God will be a place of beauty and joy in which both body and spirit are in perfect harmony. For Augustine, the felicity of the blessed will be increased by their recognition of the punishment they have escaped. They will be aware of the second death of the reprobates, and that will heighten their own gratitude and joy.[26]

The *City of God*, as Cochrane explains, represents a monumental revision of the values of antiquity. In contrast to the classical conception of an earthly order that is expected to endure (i.e., Rome as the eternal city), Augustine sees everything earthly as transient. Therefore, whoever seeks security and happiness in what is creaturely displays by that very fact the distortion of love. Whoever recognizes that security and happiness are in God alone can view with equanimity the inevitable passing of any and every earthly order.[27] To recognize that one is a sojourner and a stranger upon earth, and to believe that one's home is in the city of God, is to find a secure way of facing life's tribulations.

Augustine clearly founds his vision of the city of God on Scripture. We arrive at that city not by the dialectic of philosophers (such as Plato, in *The Republic*, advocated in his utopian vision of society) but through God's providential governance of history. To be sure, human beings cannot alter divine purpose. But from Augustine's point of view, there is room within this purpose for a moral and social progress in the human order that corresponds to a confidence that God is working out his larger purpose on the whole stage of history. Human history is a drama that exhibits the goodness of God on one hand and the diversity of individual human responses on the other. The hope of the individual is twofold: to bring into the earthly city as much of the happiness of the city of God as God permits, and ultimately to partake of the supreme happiness that belongs to the city of God alone.

# Implications of the Augustinian Image of Human Nature

Ancient Christianity attained its highest level of abstract inquiry in Augustine, whose influence has been pervasive in the West, owing largely to its roots in the Western intellectual tradition. He was a chief intellectual source of both medieval Roman Catholicism and of the Protestant Reformation. In view of the extent and importance of these two major expressions of Christianity, it's fair to say that Augustine has had a strong hand in the shaping of Western culture.

The Augustinian image of human nature radically reinterpreted the ancient classical view of human destiny wherein humankind "lived like a puppet bound to the wheel of fate. Time was thought to be circular and repetitious . . . ,"[28] like the natural course of the seasons. Humankind in general and the individual in particular "were doomed to a perpetual recurrence of the same joys, sorrows and trials. No real progress was possible."[29] Augustine presents a linear, progressive view of time and events: a beginning (creation), a climactic middle (Christ), and a goal toward which the whole of creation moves (consummation). Viewing history as the drama of divine salvation makes it possible to think of human events as unique and unrepeatable and to think of individual lives as being part of a massive, purposeful historical pattern rather than "a huge merry-go-round"[30] of eternal recurrence.

All early Christian theologians embraced some version of the drama of divine salvation. Origin, for example, held to a notion of cosmic salvation, according to which every human creature is eventually and *inevitably* saved, or drawn back to his or her Ground of being and happiness in God.[31] But Augustine's version of this drama differs from Origin's. For him, each human being must bear an element of uncertainty about his or her salvation, or personal destiny. In the course of this life, one hopes for and strives toward final happiness in God, but the ultimate attainment of this goal in the future life remains in question.

So what does Augustine's version of the drama of divine salvation mean on the personal level? It means that faith is not to be confused with certitude. Faith does not remove the ambiguities of human existence; it provides the basic thrust toward happiness in the midst of the inescapable negativities and unanswered questions of existence. Faith is the impulse toward happiness, the drive of human beings out of and beyond themselves toward the supreme end.

For all his emphasis on the consummation of history, however, Augustine does not assume that the end is at hand. The collapse of Rome does not signify the end of the world, merely the end of the pagan way of construing the world. Augustine leaves the future to the God on whose providence all things depend. In the meantime, he insists, evidence of the future city of God is given here and now, in the institution of the church. It's visible to the eyes of faith and serves as the basis of all that is worth living for.

The image of human nature that Augustine projects is perhaps best captured in a phrase by the modern French philosopher Gabriel Marcel, who speaks of the human being as *Homo viator*,[32] the pilgrim or wayfarer. To be authentically human is to lay oneself open to dissatisfaction and desire. It is the readiness to set out on the journey, to go further and further in the faithful search for God. In the course of this journey, the individual's encounter with God is a deeply personal experience that is reflected in the conscious effort to fulfill the biblical injunction to "love thy neighbor as thyself." This love of neighbor does not guarantee salvation to the person who practices it, but it does help heal the disparity between life as it often is under the will of humans and life as it ought to be and ultimately will be under the will of providence. The practice of love of neighbor is allegiance to God and alignment with his purposes.

Augustine's belief that humanity is prone to evil has frequently been interpreted as a thoroughly pessimistic view of human nature. But this interpretation discounts the stress he places on the idea of providence working out its purposes through the reform of the individual human heart (a reform Augustine knew on the basis of his own conversion experience). What is required to have a better human society is not better political institutions, but better men and women, individuals who throw in their lot with the life of faith and love.[33] We hear this motif of human betterment sounded in the following passage, where Augustine analyzes the concept of peace:

> Peace between a mortal man and his Maker consists in ordered obedience, guided by faith, under God's eternal law; peace between man and man consists in regulated fellowship. The peace of a home lies in the ordered harmony of authority and obedience between the members of a family living together. The peace of the political community is an ordered harmony of authority and obedience between citizens. The peace of the heavenly City lies in a perfectly ordered and harmonious communion of those who find their joy in God and in one another in God. Peace, in its final sense, is the calm that comes of order.[34]

Augustine does not maintain that the earthly city will or can attain the peace of the heavenly city. Unlike Plato, he does not believe in utopia. But he does suggest that humans are obligated to bring the earthly city into the similitude of the heavenly city, at least as far as it's within their capability to do so. Human beings are frail and flawed, and the attainment of perfect peace in this life escapes us. But God himself, in Christ, bestows a vision of this peace on the imagination of the peacemakers, who are the means by which the whole of human society is leavened.

# Suggestions for Discussion and Study

1.  Augustine developed his idea of predestination in opposition to Pelagius, a British monk who affirmed the inalienable power of human nature to do what is right. At bottom, Pelagius taught that the individual can assure his or her own salvation through perseverance in good works. The church rejected the teachings of Pelagius at a general synod in Carthage in 418, but this rejection did not mean the acceptance of everything Augustine taught about predestination. The opponents of Augustine's idea maintained that it undercut moral incentive; there would be no reason for being moral if one were confident of one's salvation, and likewise no reason if one lacked this confidence. It was an idea that could lead either to conceited optimism about personal destiny or to resigned pessimism. To get a notion of how Augustine responded to such criticism, read his treatises *On Grace and Free Will* and *On Rebuke and Grace*. Before doing that, though, speculate on what answer one might give to the proposition that if personal destiny is worked out in advance by some power beyond us, there is really no room for meaningful personal response. What was the Sophoclean answer to this proposition? Is Augustine's similar, or radically different?

2.  In what basic ways does Augustine's concept of history differ from the ancient classical concept?

3.  How does Augustine's concept of justice differ from Plato's?

4. One view of Christianity is that it upholds the status quo by urging human beings to be content with their unhappy lot in this world and to look forward to happiness in the next. Certain features of Augustine's thought support this view, but others challenge it. What are these other features? On what grounds, if any, would Augustine advocate social change?

5. Augustine offers a major Christian image of human nature. If you were asked to summarize the Augustinian image in one hundred words, what would you say?

6. Augustine lived fifteen hundred years ago. What are the strengths and weaknesses of the Augustinian image of human nature for today?

7. If our age is marked by a quest for scientific certainty, what might Augustine have to say about the nature of this quest?

# Further Reading

Battenhouse, Roy W., ed. *A Companion to the Study of St. Augustine.* New York: Oxford University Press, 1956. A collection of essays by various scholars on many aspects of Augustine's thought.

Bourke, Vernon J., ed. *The Essential Augustine.* Indianapolis: Hackett Publishing Co., 1978. Presents a wide sampling of Augustine's writings under the headings of major topics.

Brown, Peter. *Augustine of Hippo.* Berkeley: University of California Press, 1969. A highly authoritative biography of Augustine against the background of the fourth century.

# Notes

1. Augustine, *The Confessions of St. Augustine,* trans., with introduction and notes, John K. Ryan (Garden City, NY: Doubleday & Co., Image Books, 1960), bk. 8, chap. 12, par. 29. (All quotations from Augustine's *Confessions* are from this edition. Various translations of Augustine's works exist, but not all are readily available. To facilitate location of passages from Augustine in different editions, passages are cited here by book, chapter, and paragraph divisions, standard in most translations of Augustine.)

2. Plato, *Phaedo*, trans. Hugh Tredennick, in *Plato: The Collected Dialogues*, ed. Edith Hamilton and Huntinton Cairns (Princeton, NJ: Princeton University Press, 1973), par. 99c.
3. Plato, *The Republic*, trans. Paul Shorey, in *Plato: The Collected Dialogues*, op. cit., bk. 6, par. 508–509.
4. Augustine, *Of True Religion*, in *Augustine: Earlier Writings*, trans. and ed. John H. S. Burleigh, The Library of Christian Classics, vol. 6 (Philadelphia: The Westminster Press, 1953), chap. 29, par. 72.
5. Augustine, *The Teacher*, in *Augustine: Earlier Writings*, op. cit., chap. 11, par. 38.
6. Etienne Gilson, *The Christian Philosophy of Saint Augustine* (New York: Random House, 1960), pp. 27–37.
7. Augustine, *Eighty-Three Different Questions*, trans. David L. Mosher, *The Fathers of the Church: A New Translation*, vol. 70 (Washington, D.C.: The Catholic University of America Press, 1982), par. 48.
8. Augustine, *The Confessions*, op. cit., bk. 10, chap. 6, par. 10.
9. Theodore Roethke, "The Waking," *The Collected Poems of Theodore Roethke* (Garden City, New York: Doubleday & Co., Inc., 1966), p. 108.
10. Plato, *Protagoras*, trans. W. K. C. Guthrie, in *Plato: The Collected Dialogues*, op. cit., par. 352a-c.
11. Augustine, *The Confessions*, op. cit., bk. 2, chap. 4, par. 9.
12. Ibid.
13. Augustine, *On Free Will*, in *Augustine: Earlier Writings*, op. cit., bk. 2, chap. 20, par. 54.
14. Augustine, "Seventh Homily," *Homilies on I John*, trans. John Burnaby, in *Augustine: Later Works*, vol. 8 (Philadelphia: The Westminster Press, 1955), par. 8.
15. Anders Nygren, *Agape and Eros*, trans. Philip S. Watson (New York: Harper & Row, Publishers, Harper Torchbooks, 1969), p. 478.
16. Augustine, "Second Discourse on Psalm 31," in *Augustine on the Psalms*, trans. and annot. Dame Scholastic Hebgin and Dame Felicitas Corrigan, 2 vols., *Ancient Christian Writers: The Works of the Fathers in Translation*, no. 30 (London: Longmans, Green and Co., 1961), 2: par. 5.
17. Ibid.
18. Augustine, *The Literal Meaning of Genesis*, trans. and annot. John Hammond Taylor, S. J., 2 vols., *Ancient Christian Writers: The Works of the Fathers in Translation*, no. 42 (New York: Newman Press, 1982), 2: bk. 11, chap. 15, par. 20.
19. Charles Norris Cochrane, *Christianity and Classical Culture: A Study of Thought and Action from Augustus to Augustine* (London: Oxford University Press, 1968), pp. 48–56.
20. Augustine, *The City of God*, trans. John Healey, 2 vols. (London: J. M. Dent & Sons, Ltd., 1957), 2: bk. 15. (All references to *The City of God* relate to this edition, except where otherwise noted.)
21. Augustine, *The City of God*, op. cit., 1: bk. 4, chap. 4.
22. Ibid., 2: bk. 19, chap. 17.
23. Ibid., 2: bk. 20.
24. Hannah Arendt, *The Life of the Mind*, 2 vols. (New York: Harcourt Brace Jovanovich, 1978), 2: 105.
25. Augustine, *The City of God*, op. cit., 2: bk. 22, chap. 20.

26. Ibid., 2: bk. 21, chap. 23.
27. Cochrane, op. cit., pp. 456–516.
28. Vernon J. Bourke, *Wisdom from St. Augustine* (Houston, TX: Center for Thomistic Studies, 1984), p. 194.
29. Ibid.
30. Ibid.
31. Allan D. Galloway, *The Cosmic Christ* (London: Nisbet & Co., Ltd., 1951), pp. 87–90.
32. Gabriel Marcel, *Homo Viator: Introduction to a Metaphysic of Hope*, trans. Emma Craufurd (New York: Harper & Brothers, Harper Torchbooks, 1962), p. 11.
33. Bourke, op. cit., p. 195.
34. Augustine, *The City of God*, trans. Gerald G. Walsh, S. J., Demetrius B. Zema, S. J., Grace Monahan, O. S. U., ed., Vernon J. Bourke (Garden City, NY: Doubleday & Co., Inc., Image Books, 1958), bk. 19, chap. 13.

# ·4·

# THOMAS HOBBES
## and the image of
# EGOISM

# Cultural Background

The death of Augustine marked the end of the ancient world in the West and the beginning of the ten centuries of the Middle Ages. When historians speak of the end of the ancient world, they mean the Roman Empire crumbled, and waves of barbarian peoples inundated Europe. The ancient monolithic unity—similar to that which we see in the Asian Communist world of today—disintegrated.

Three cultures—Byzantine, Muslim, and Western—developed within Europe between 500 and 1100. Whereas Western culture by far dominated the largest area in Europe, the other two were considerably superior in social and intellectual achievements during this period. Greek science was transmitted to Europe through Byzantine compilers, and the Muslims transmitted Aristotelian thought through translations from Greek into Syriac, then from Syriac into Arabic and, sometimes, Hebrew and Latin.

In Spain, between 900 and 1100, Muslims, Christians, and Jews mingled and fashioned an extraordinary culture of different faiths whose learning, literature, art, industry, and trade enticed many scholars and tradesmen to travel across the Pyrenees to places such as Seville and Cordoba. In this way, as well as by less traceable means, Muslim learning and science spread to the north.

Centers of learning—which were forerunners of medieval universities—began to appear in monasteries and cathedrals, such as those at Monte Casino, Cluny, Chartres, York, and Canterbury. The knowledge taught in these centers became known as *scholasticism*, that is, theology, philosophy, and the seven liberal arts: arithmetic, geometry, astronomy, music, grammar, logic, and rhetoric.

Scholasticism was rooted in the philosophical ideas of Plato and Aristotle, ideas sifted, adapted, and absorbed through many centuries. It offered massive intellectual support for a religious vision of the universe as a hierarchical order. Thomas Aquinas (1225–1274), whose *Summae* are inclusive scholastic summaries, posits a universe with God at the top, then the higher intelligences (the angels) of pure form without matter, then human beings, composed of form and matter.

Upon this vision of hierarchical order medieval cathedrals were conceived. These massive structures reminded the medieval beholder of his or her own place in an orderly, purposeful universe. Inside them the beholder could sense Augustine's city of God on earth and then readily imagine the higher level of the heavenly city.

Between 1100 and 1350, scholasticism represented a coherent, authoritative Christian worldview, dramatically rendered by the greatest of medieval poets, Dante Alighieri (1265–1321), in *The Divine Comedy*.

This period, besides witnessing the height of medieval culture, also saw the introduction of numerous forces that were to produce vast changes in European society in later periods. Among these forces were the rise of commerce, industry, town life, and banking. Toward the end of the Middle Ages, prominent scholars increasingly rejected the schema of scholasticism in favor of a freer mode of learning called *humanism*.

Humanism originated in the Renaissance, that period in Western culture spanning roughly the fifteenth and sixteenth centuries. It started as a revival of interest in philosophical and literary texts of ancient Greece and Rome. In the fifteenth century, the Turkish conquest of Constantinople propelled Byzantine scholars who spoke Greek (a language Europe had forgotten) to migrate to Mediterranean Europe, where they found Italian scholars ready for and receptive to classical learning.

The renewal of this learning had far reaching implications. For one thing, the textual scholarship that accompanied it undercut ecclesiastical authority. Roman Lorenzo Valla (c. 1405–1457), for example, used textual scholarship to show that Jerome's translation of the Bible, the *Vulgate*, which was the authorized version of the Roman Church, was inaccurate and that the Donation of Constantine, which bestowed broad political powers upon the Pope, was a forgery. Humanism in fifteenth-century Italy planted seeds that would manifest themselves in the Protestant Reformation of sixteenth-century Germany.

Through its revival of classical thought, humanism introduced a philosophical attitude that conflicted with the prevailing worldview of medieval Christianity. In opposition to the medieval view that life on earth is a preparation for eternity, humanism offered the view that life on earth is an end in itself. Humanist thinkers displayed great confidence in the capacity of the human race to manage its own destiny. A typical expression of this confidence occurs in *Oration on the Dignity of Man*, by Pico della Mirandola (1463–1494), wherein he imagines God passing the responsibility for the future of the world over to humanity, saying,

> We have made thee neither of heaven nor of earth, neither mortal nor immortal, so that with freedom of choice and with honor, as though the maker and molder of thyself, thou mayest fashion thyself in whatever shape thou shalt prefer.[1]

Renaissance humanism reasserted the ancient classical notion of the human creature as an autonomous, rational being, rather than as a creature wholly submissive to God.

The Renaissance was not limited solely to literary and philosophical activity, nor was it committed simply to the revival of classical learning. The intellectual temper of the Renaissance inevitably prompted a new mode of analyzing the structure of physical nature. With studies of human anatomy by Leonardo da Vinci (1452–1519), with investigations in astronomy by Nicolaus Copernicus (1473–1543) and Johannes Kepler (1571–1630), with discoveries in mechanics by Galileo Galilei (1564–1642), together with the work of many others, natural science was born in its modern form, with its stress upon observation and mathematics.

In some respects the term *renaissance* ("rebirth") is inappropriate. Not only a rebirth, it was a new birth in humanity's long philosophical gestation. While it revived many ideas from the classical world, it also launched humanity on creative paths in the arts, sciences, and philosophy that outran anything previously anticipated. It was a vital, expansive cultural age, which we speak of today as the beginning of the modern world. As a late Renaissance thinker, therefore, Thomas Hobbes had his feet in two worlds: the ancient and the modern.

# Biography

Hobbes was born in Malmesbury, Wiltshire, England, in 1588. Elizabeth I was on the throne, and England was at war with

Spain. In an autobiography written in Latin verse in his old age, Hobbes refers to his premature birth when his mother heard of the approach of the Spanish Armada: *Ut pareret geminos, meque metumque simul*[2] ("Fear and I were born twins"). Hobbes' long life spanned most of the seventeenth century, a period of English history that afforded many a citizen sufficient grounds for fear.

Five years after Hobbes' birth, the reign of the Tudors ended with the death of Elizabeth, and the reign of the Stuarts began with James I. At the end of the rule of James I, opposition to the king and his Royalists was active in Parliament. This opposition was in the hands of the Puritans, persons who rated the authority of the Bible and their consciences above that of the magistrates, bishops, and counselors to the king. Puritan demands for a greater share in government ultimately led to the Civil War, the beheading of Charles I, and the establishment of the Protectorate government under Oliver Cromwell. The Stuart monarchy was reinstated under Charles II with the Restoration of 1660, and the Royalists regained power. It is no exaggeration to say, consequently, that the England of Hobbes' day was in a constant state of political and social turmoil that often amounted to terror.

Hobbes' father was a clergyman whose life was complicated by a lack of education, a quarrelsome disposition, and poverty. An uncle took charge of the boy's education: till he was fourteen, Hobbes attended school at Malmesbury, where he distinguished himself by translating Euripides' *Medea* into Latin, and at age fifteen, he entered Magdalen College, Oxford.

Hobbes graduated at the end of five years at Oxford, and became a tutor in the family of William Cavendish, later the Earl of Devonshire. This position in the Cavendish family lasted many years and was one of the great formative influences of his life. In 1610 it became his duty to accompany the son and heir of the family on a grand tour of Europe. During this year-long tour, Hobbes studied French and Italian and made contacts with persons of position and learning. It occurred to him that his years at Oxford had not been very productive, and he resolved to remedy deficiencies in his formal education through intense independent study.

Returning to England from the Continent, Hobbes became a part-time secretary to Francis Bacon (1561–1626) who, as statesman, performed legal duties for the monarchy. Additionally, Hobbes participated in social events attended by literary notables, and his intellectual horizons were greatly expanded thereby. In 1628 he published a translation of the *Eight Books of the Peloponnesian War* by Thucydides, the Greek historian with whom Hobbes shared a sense of the perils of democracy. This work was favorably received and helped to establish him as a man of letters.

In that same year, Hobbes' tutorship with the Cavendish family was temporarily interrupted, and he was confronted with the need to seek employment elsewhere. He thus transferred his services (and made another tour of the Continent) as tutor-companion to the son of Sir Gervase Clinton. During this second tour Hobbes discovered Euclid, an event that is recorded by John Aubrey in his *Brief Lives*.

> Being in a Gentleman's Library, Euclid's Elements lay open, and 'twas the 47 *El. libri I*. He read the Proposition. *By G—*, sayd he (he would now and then sweare an emphaticall Oath by way of emphasis) *this is impossible!* So he reads the Demonstration of it, which referred him back to such a Proposition; which proposition he read. That referred him back to another, which he also read. *Et sic deinceps* [and so on] that at last he was demonstratively convinced of that trueth. This made him in love with Geometry.[3]

This discovery of Euclid, when Hobbes was forty, stands as a milestone in his life, for it awakened in him a passion for the possibilities latent in mathematics, particularly geometry. Hobbes was both by temperament and choice a *rationalist*, one who assumes that by connecting ideas consciously, coherently, and purposefully, we can arrive at intellectual certainty. He thought he perceived in geometry the very dictates of rationality laid bare, and it thus became for him the model for the pursuit of all knowledge.

In 1630 Hobbes returned to the service of the Cavendish family, and from 1634 to 1636 he toured the Continent a third time. His protégé was again the son of the Cavendish Earl with whom he had toured in 1610. In Paris, Hobbes became well acquainted with the French philosopher Father Marin Mersenne (1588–1648)—friend and correspondent of René Descartes (1596–1650), who was the center of an intellectual circle committed to advancing the great mathematical and scientific discoveries of the age. Hobbes made a special journey to Italy in 1636 to meet Galileo, whose ideas were to profoundly impress his own thought.

Hobbes went back to England in 1637, but seeing the country was on the verge of civil war, and fearing for his own safety (having engaged in the controversies of politics through his writings), he returned to the Continent in 1640 and spent the next eleven years in France and Holland.

It was during this period that he conceived a philosophical work in three parts, dealing in turn with matter, or physical nature, with human nature, and with society. In fulfilling this plan, however, he changed the order in which he had intended to work on it. In response to the mounting political crisis in England between Charles I and the Puritans, Hobbes wrote on society first in an effort to set forth a philosophy for political peace. Thus, *De Cive* (*"Society"*) was published in 1642, *De Corpore* (*"Physical Nature"*) in 1655, and *De Homine* (*"Human Nature"*) in 1657. What we recognize today as most important in these three works, Hobbes managed to consolidate in *Leviathan*, published in 1651.

The *Leviathan* was soon acclaimed as a masterpiece of political thought on the order of Plato's *The Republic* or Machiavelli's *The Prince*. But just as his fame grew, so did resentment against him. Anti-traditionalist elements in Hobbes' work, especially those pertaining to religion, made him intensely unpopular with the legitimist and church-minded Royalists, as well as French clergymen. Fearing an attack on his life, he hastened back to England and threw himself upon the mercy of the Puritan regime. Cromwell, as ruler of this regime, had become so powerful that he and Hobbes, who philosophically advocated the idea of a powerful ruler, had a good deal in common. Cromwell allowed him to reside in England, where he lived out his last twenty-eight years.

In the eyes of many Puritans, Hobbes was a Royalist by association, if not by loyalty. Had the Puritan regime continued, it's likely he would eventually have found himself officially persecuted. But when Cromwell died in 1658, reaction against the Puritan regime had set in, and then the Restoration came. The restoration of the monarchy proved fortunate for Hobbes. He had served as tutor to Charles II when the latter—then Prince of Wales—was a young man living in France. Charles had a fondness for his old tutor, giving him a pension and generally guaranteeing his welfare. So, at the age of seventy-two, a person of fame, means, and security, Hobbes entered the final phase of his remarkable career.

Constrained by the king from engaging in further political writing (though he did manage to write *Behemoth*, a history of the Civil War) Hobbes concentrated on other subjects. During the last nineteen years of his life he produced a succession of works on mathematical and physical subjects that reveal his strong scientific temper. He also returned to his early interest in classical literature, and eighty-seven produced complete translations of Homer's *Iliad* and *Odyssey*.

Though Hobbes wrote on an impressive range of subjects, he's best remembered for his speculations on the organization of society, ideas that hold an important place in the history of political thought. Thus, we can hardly discuss Hobbes without bringing them into play. In this book, however, we're not so much trying to master the intricacies of his political philosophy as to delineate the image of human nature he projects.

## Hobbes on What Can I Know?

Hobbes' theory of knowledge is intimately related to his metaphysical vision of the universe as a gigantic machine constructed of material bodies and operated in accordance with principles that the mind has the ability to recognize. As we have noted earlier, Hobbes was deeply influenced by Galileo, whose vision of the universe embraced physical laws such as the law of gravitation and the law that a moving body will continue its movement unless prevented by external interference. For Hobbes, all inanimate things and all life may be pictured in light of physical laws.

In the universe, bodies inhabit space and have certain attributes, or accidents, such as movement, rest, cold, heat, color, hardness, softness. At the center of everything he conceives *motion*, a term Hobbes uses at times to mean movement and at other times to mean the law of cause and effect. In the sense of cause and effect (Hobbes' predominant meaning), motion is a body's continuous giving up of one space and assuming another. When one body affects another, it either generates an accident in the affected body or destroys an accident.

Let's say, for example, that a billiard ball is at rest on a table. When it's struck by a second ball, the first ball is no longer at rest but in motion. In this case, the second ball has destroyed the accident of rest in the first and caused the accident of movement. The whole of reality, for Hobbes, is a *plenum*, a space, every part of which is filled with moving matter.

So, while he is a rationalist, he is also a *materialist*, i.e., one who perceives the universe in terms of the mechanical operation of its parts upon each other. In this mechanistic universe, Hobbes asks, what is the human being if not a machine? "For what is the *heart*, but a *spring*: and the *nerves*, but so many *strings*; and the *joints*, but so many *wheels*, giving motion to the whole body?"[4]

Over the last three centuries, the Hobbesian view of the human being as a machine has become ingrained in Western thinking. Physiology, molecular biology, brain chemistry, behaviorist psychology, and other areas of modern science are indebted to it. These sciences offer more or less mechanistic accounts of the behavioral foundations we have in common with other creatures. One of the basic problems that confronts any mechanistic account of the human being, however, whether it be that of Hobbes or some contemporary thinker, is to explain what distinguishes the human being from creatures such as rats, guinea pigs, and monkeys. If, like these creatures, the human being is a machine, what distinguishes the human machine from any other?

Hobbes insists that what distinguishes us from other creatures is our capacity to reason. What exactly, then, is *reason*? He builds his answer to this question by dealing first with other major concepts: *sensation, imagination, memory, experience, names* (words), and *language*. Let's touch upon these concepts individually as they lead up to Hobbes' concept of reason.

All of the complicated processes of thought, Hobbes maintains, involve vast numbers of sense impressions, or *sensation*. The thought process begins when a body or physical thing external to us moves and causes a motion inside of us, as when we see a tree, for example. Seeing the tree is a perception or sensation.

Long after the initial impact, we retain the sensation of the external thing within us, just "as we see in the water, though the wind cease, the waves give not over rolling for a long time after."[5] This retention, Hobbes insists, is what we mean by *imagination*, which is simply a lingering or "decaying" sensation. Later, when we want to express this decay and indicate that the sense is fading, we call this *memory*. All of our fading memories, in turn, add up to what we call *experience*.[6]

Thought manifests itself, therefore, in varying ways and is recognizable under varying labels. But the idea Hobbes stresses is that every thought has "been begotten upon the organs of sense."[7] Thought finds its data *there*, immediately given to it in sensation as soon as it begins to operate theoretically.

A pressing question, then, is how we become aware of our sensations. What are the means by which we know what we experience? We know what we experience, Hobbes tells us, by virtue of our ability to formulate *names*[8] to mark our sensations. To illustrate this Hobbesian notion, let's imagine we are standing in bright sunlight. Our eyes may hurt, but we pay little attention till we form the name "pain." It wasn't that we had repressed the pain; we simply hadn't noticed it before we'd given it a name. From Hobbes' point of view, names are not devices by which pre-existent knowledge is expressed; they are an activity prior to knowledge itself, without which knowledge would not be possible.

This activity of marking sensations with names, however, is not identical with language itself, which is a social activity. When names are linked one to the other in language, that language mirrors our thoughts (which rise from our experience) and allows us to "show to others that knowledge which we have attained."[9] A main function of language is to "demonstrate or approve our reckonings to other men."[10] This ability to string thoughts together in names and to construct arguments is what Hobbes means by the process of *ratiocination*, or reason. For him, reason raises human beings above the nature of beasts.

Parts of Hobbes' work read like a dictionary, attempting to establish at every turn the precise definition of terms. This method of writing may test the patience of the reader, but for Hobbes it is a necessary feature of the attempt to "approve our reckonings to other men."[11] He writes:

> Seeing . . . that truth consisteth in the right ordering of names in our affirmations, a man that seeketh precise truth had need to remember what every name he uses stands for, and to place it accordingly, or else he will find himself

entangled in words, as a bird in lime twigs, the more he struggles the more belimed. And therefore in geometry, which is the only science that it hath pleased God hitherto to bestow on mankind, men begin at settling the significations of their words; which settling of significations they call *definitions*, and place them in the beginning of their reckoning.[12]

Hobbes is convinced that the failure to begin with definitions is a serious flaw in the thinking process. It accounts for misunderstanding and confusion at all levels of thought. Writers often combine and use names and phrases in sentences that are blatantly meaningless. To choose one of Hobbes' own examples: "*inpoured virtue*"; as though, he says scoffingly, "virtue can be poured."[13] Hobbes maintains that scholastic thought thrived on such verbal ambiguities. His aim is to put things on an unambiguous footing by beginning the thinking process (as the geometrician does) with definitions. In Hobbes, the question What can I know? takes on a definitely linguistic character. We can only claim to have knowledge of that which we can unambiguously communicate.

Because we can only claim knowledge of what we can unambiguously communicate, morality, from the Hobbesian perspective, becomes a problematic area of human life. Morality is that area where our judgments are greatly affected by our personal dispositions; it is also that area where ambiguous language flourishes because we tend to use names to mean different things in different contexts. Our moral names, Hobbes points out,

> which besides the signification of what we imagine of their nature, have a signification also of the nature, disposition, and interest of the speaker; such as are the names of virtues and vices; for one man calleth *wisdom*, what another calleth *fear*; and one *cruelty*, what another *justice*; one *prodigality*, what another *magnanimity*; and one *gravity*, what another *stupidity*, &c. And therefore such names can never be true grounds of any ratiocination.[14]

Hobbes' observations about the ambiguity of the language of morality reveal a paradox at the very center of his work. On the one hand, he assumes that we can have knowledge of the physical world, or nature, because our thoughts about it can be clearly defined, communicated, and verified in relation to the experience of others. On the other hand, he assumes that we cannot have knowledge of morality because our thoughts about it cannot be clearly defined, communicated, and verified in relation to the experience of others. The individual human being can indeed define his or her moral thoughts, but such definition is ruled by the individual's own constitution, needs, and history in a way that his or her definition of nature is not.

Another way to express this paradox is to say that for Hobbes the language of nature is rational and dependable, while the language of morality is irrational and nondependable. He assumes we can trust one another when we are speaking about nature, but we cannot trust one another when we are speaking about morality. It's as though two thinkers reside in Hobbes at once: one who recognizes the rational side of human nature, and the other who recognizes the irrational side. When Hobbes sets forth his theory of morality, as we will see, it's this thinker who recognizes the irrational side of human nature who dramatically steps forward.

## Hobbes on What Ought I to Do?

Hobbes' theory of morality involves the same kind of mechanistic explanation we saw in his theory of knowledge. He begins by insisting that all human conduct has its origin in sensation. All humans—by virtue of the external stimuli that affect their sensory apparatus—share two kinds of activity: one that Hobbes calls *vital*, the other *voluntary*. Humans not only live, they will. What they will to do is a product of their ability to think, to imagine. Hobbes calls this voluntary action *endeavor*; such action originates in a human being's natural urge for survival.

Endeavor toward something, Hobbes continues, is *appetite* and away from something, *aversion*. These two aspects of endeavor account for human dispositions in relation to objects and persons; they have the same meanings as the names *love* and *hate*. Humans love what they think will help them survive, and they hate what they judge to be a threat to their survival. Human beings are fundamentally egoistic, or self-centered. The names *good* and *evil* mean whatever each individual ascribes to them; individuals call whatever they love good and whatever they hate evil.[15] If it's possible to generalize about human loves and hates, it's simply this: Life itself is the referent of value. What enlarges and enriches life is good; what diminishes and endangers life is evil.

Hobbes conceives of an original stage of nature—a prehistorical epoch—when humans lived strictly according to their loves and hates. It's of no great importance to Hobbes' argument to know whether human beings ever *did* live in such a state of nature. He's actually theorizing about how humans *would* live if their appetites and aversions, loves and hates, were thoroughly and generally displayed.

Conflict or quarrel would mark all human relations in this state of nature. There are three basic "causes of quarrel" among human beings, Hobbes declares: First, "competition," because we all seek our own survival; second, "diffidence," because competition leads to mistrust of others; and third, "glory," because we all desire others to value us as we value ourselves, and we're quick to regard any slight as a sign of contempt. The first cause of quarrel, Hobbes adds, "maketh men invade [or assail one another] for gain; the second, for safety; and the third, for reputation."[16]

In Hobbes' original state of nature, no individual would have security against any other individual apart from that provided by his or her strength and intelligence. And since, as Hobbes contends, every individual possesses essentially the same bodily and mental capacities as any other individual, the degree of security enjoyed by even the strongest and most intelligent would not be worth much. (Even the physically weak could master the strong through trickery.) So, in this state of nature, constant and unending quarrel would be the human lot—a "war of every man against every man."[17] There'd be no cooperation, and hence "no arts; no letters; no society; and which is worst of all, continual fear, and danger of violent death; and the life of man, solitary, poor, nasty, brutish, and short."[18]

Hobbes thus offers a grim picture of the human condition. Nor is this picture wholly a product of his fancy. He lived in a period (similar in many ways to our own) of political and religious struggles and witnessed the clash of powerful historical forces. He saw social customs and institutions change violently and attributed this change to the very principles he outlined as causing quarrels among human beings in the state of nature: competition, diffidence, and glory. In portraying the state of nature, Hobbes is also portraying the existing state of society he knew from personal experience. He is speaking essentially about war. Perhaps nobody has offered a more discriminating definition of the concept of war than Hobbes:

> For WAR, consisteth not in battle only, or the act of fighting; but in a tract of time, wherein the will to contend by battle is sufficiently known: and therefore the notion of *time*, is to be considered in the nature of war; as it is in the nature of weather. For as the nature of foul weather, lieth not in a shower or two of rain; but in an inclination thereto of many days together: so the nature of war, consisteth not in actual fighting; but in the known disposition thereto, during all the time there is no assurance to the contrary. All other time is PEACE.[19]

Pessimistic as Hobbes may seem, he does hold out the possibility of humanity's overcoming the predicament in which it finds itself in the state of nature. By facing the sorry fact of our warlike nature, we can turn this fact to our advantage. Every human being lives in fear of every other human being, Hobbes declares, and this fear in itself is potentially inventive, for it can prompt us to seek ways of providing against what is feared. Knowing that continual war with our neighbor is a threat to our personal survival, we can decide, for our own good, to seek peace with our neighbor as far as there is hope to attain it. Thus, Hobbes recommends that we make agreements with our neighbor as a means of establishing our own well-being.

Let's picture how this Hobbesian notion of making an agreement might manifest in actual practice. Suppose there were three gold prospectors in a deserted mountain area, each of whom had independently discovered the same rich lode of gold. Each prospector is trying to acquire as much gold for himself as possible before the lode is exhausted. Each, in effect, is competing with the other two. Not only is acquiring the gold a problem, so is keeping it. Each prospector is afraid to turn his back or sleep for fear one or both of the other prospectors will overcome him and steal what he has so arduously worked to acquire.

Now, this fear provokes in the prospectors an idea for a solution to their mutual problem. It dawns upon them—fear having awakened their thinking power—that the most likely way of surviving and profiting from their work is to agree to renounce violence against one another (since every person, according to Hobbes, has a natural right to violence as a means of self-preservation) and to compile the gold. Whereas no one prospector will get all of it, at least each will get an equal share.

The agreement is struck, but there's still a problem. For, given the egoistic nature that Hobbes sees in all of us, there's no reason for any one of the prospectors to keep his word if he can devise a way to overcome the others, steal their gold, and make a clean escape. There's still every reason for the prospectors to distrust one another. In spite of the agreement, none yet dares to sleep.

The reasonable solution is to introduce still another party into the picture, who we'll call the authority. The three prospectors not only give this authority all of the gold to divide as he or she sees fit, they also yield to him or her their natural right to violence as a means of self-preservation. They also agree that the authority should have police powers. In effect, this authority (which Hobbes calls variously the *sovereign*, the *commonwealth*, or the *state*) now wields absolute power, which, in accepting, he or she agrees to use to guarantee that the prospectors honor their agreement with one another. The prospectors, in other words, have bound themselves—for purposes of peace and self-preservation—to what Hobbes regards as the *contract*.[20]

The social contract, as Hobbes envisions it, isn't something human beings arrive at gladly, but by a grudging, mutual forbearance. Nor is making this contract without risk, for who or what is to guarantee that the authority, being merely human, will not abuse the power that he or she has come to possess? But even with this risk, as Hobbes reasons, living by contract under even an imperious authority is preferable to living in a continual state of war. Indeed, the most pertinent reason Hobbes can imagine for not obeying the authority is if he or she proves impotent in enforcing the social contract. In such a situation, individuals must revert to their own defenses, as in the original state of nature. Submission to authority is the price humans pay in order to guarantee the safety of their lives and possessions.

Hobbes' answer to What ought I to do? is simply that the individual ought to obey existing authority without asking any questions or making any difficulties. The reason individuals ought to do this is straightforward: there's a high probability that in disobeying authority they'll lose more than they'll gain. The underlying motive of human conduct, Hobbes insists, is always some benefit to the self. It's in the private interest of the individual to prevent the miseries of war. In disobeying authority—which is to say, by violating the directives by which the social contract is enforced—the individual contributes to the recurrence of anarchy and thereby undercuts his or her own security. To say it's in the individual's interest to obey authority is equivalent to saying it's the individual's duty. Individuals owe it to themselves to obey authority since by no other way—given the rudimentary fact of humanity's egoistic, predatory nature—is it possible to advance the individual's urgent claim to life.

For the sake of clarity, it's important to assert that Hobbes' theory of morality does not rest, finally, on a notion of rigid authoritarianism; it rests on a notion of radical self-interest. So fundamental are the demands of self-interest in human make-up that even so-called sympathetic acts, wherein concern is expressed for others, have an ultimate basis in self-interest. Hobbes offers a paraphrase of the Golden Rule: "*Do not that to another, which thou wouldest not have done to thyself.*"[21]

But the Hobbesian evocation of a biblical precept in no way softens his doctrine of egoism. As he sees it, human beings are so constituted by nature that they simply *cannot* act other than in their own self-interest. If we show sympathy toward others it's because we want some return for the sympathy we've shown. We give of ourselves in order to put others in our debt and to manipulate them into giving us what we want. Regardless of how overtly unselfish his or her acts seem to be, the individual is driven by uncontrollable self-interest.

Earlier, we suggested that Hobbes sees reason as the distinguishing trait of human nature. Having surveyed his theory of morality, however, we can now see that the human being is also irrational, a creature driven by egoistic desires. In fact, our egoism, our self-interest awakens the power of reason, the instrument by which we get what we want, security, and avoid what we do not want, death.

# Hobbes on
# for What Can I Hope?

*Leviathan* is written in four parts, titled, in order of their occurrence, "Of Man," "Of Commonwealth," "Of a Christian Commonwealth," and "Of the Kingdom of Darkness." The last two parts, constituting half the pages of the total work, are devoted to the subject of religion. They excited more interest and controversy in Hobbes' time than they do in ours. So provocative were his ideas on the subject of religion that, for many of his contemporaries, his name became synonymous with atheism.

Atheist or not, Hobbes kept up the appearance of being a Christian and examined religious topics seriously. For him, the most urgent issue was the relationship between church and state. He saw in the competing religious loyalties of his day a constant threat to civil peace; he proposed, as a means of minimizing this threat, the establishment of an official state church (he favored the Anglican church), with the sovereign as its head. In effect, Hobbes wanted to bring religion under the control of the state. "This is the generation," he says, "of that great LEVIATHAN, or rather . . . of that *mortal* god to which we owe . . . our peace and defence."[22] Hobbes borrows the term Leviathan from the fortieth and forty-first chapters of the book of Job, where Leviathan is a fierce monster no one can attack and still be safe. Hobbes' Leviathan is the sovereign, or state. It's to this "mortal god" that the individual owes the conditions of "peace and defence" that make human happiness possible.

We can shed light on Hobbes' idea of human happiness by comparing it with Augustine's. Both thinkers assume that human appetites, or desires, are insatiable. For Augustine, our desires can never be satisfied by the things of this world; desire presses us onward to the eternal happiness of the next world. For Hobbes, there is no next world; so we might as well derive from this world whatever happiness it affords, pursuing the objects of our desire to the utmost. While we live, Hobbes says, we have desires, and desire presupposes endless goals. "Seeing all *delight* is *appetite*, and presupposeth a further end, there can be *no contentment* but in *proceeding*. . . . *Felicity*, therefore, by which we mean continual delight, consisteth *not* in *having* prospered but in *prospering*."[23] If for Augustine this process of "prospering" is nothing but an endless cycle of emotional torment, for Hobbes it is the chief way life advances in happiness.

For Hobbes there is no *summum bonum*, one supreme good that is the rightful goal of human happiness. He does indicate that all human beings ought to seek peace rather than war, but for him peace is not an end in itself; it's simply that season of time in which humans are freest (because they are most secure) to pursue the objects of their personal desires. Hobbes does not prescribe what the objects of desire ought to be. As he sees it, individuals are free to pursue whatever objects hold the promise of happiness, providing this pursuit does not encroach on the neighbor's freedom to pursue the objects of his or her desire. A primary function of the state is to safeguard against such encroachment. It authoritatively regulates the self-interest of the individual in order to permit limited but secure expression of the insistent desires of all. If human beings are to have any significant hope of happiness, Hobbes insists, they must be willing to submit to the authority of Leviathan, the only power capable of keeping the potentially destructive forces of human nature in check.

## Implications of the Hobbesian Image of Human Nature

The image of human nature that Hobbes projects is one of a solitary individual who is propelled by egoism into conflict with all other creatures of his or her own kind. It's not an image that flatters, but we can hardly accuse Hobbes of deliberate cynicism. He describes human nature as he genuinely sees it and draws political implications from what he sees. The whole line of Hobbes' political thought represents an extreme development of the idea of the egoism of humanity. Somehow, he insists, this egoism, and the violence it engenders, must be curbed if there is to be any peace, knowledge, arts, letters, crafts, customs—those artifices of culture separating humanity from the state of nature.

In the interest of the betterment of humanity, Hobbes sets forth the notion that any government is preferable to no government, and the best government is authoritarian. But the Hobbesian notion of government implies the trading of one kind of enslavement for another. The individual might feel secure, but at what cost? For Hobbes, remember, the human being is a creature of passionate intensity who thrives on achieving one goal after the other. A main function of government is to thwart this intensity. One can imagine in the Hobbesian state the life of the individual being severely restricted and oppressively dull.

An even more solemn problem attends Hobbes' notion of authoritarian government. In the modern world, especially in the twentieth century, the Hobbesian Leviathan has come to life, not merely in theory but in fact. Cambodia under Pol Pot, Russia under Stalin, and Germany under Hitler all represent states where the absolute authority of government resulted in the calculated annihilation of millions of those states' own citizens. There is no reason to assume that the individual has any less to fear from the violence of the state than from the violence of the neighbor.

What must be said for Hobbes himself, however, is that he was no warmonger or militarist, nor did he foresee that mass murder in the form of pogroms and genocidal crusades would become part of the inner dynamic of modern Leviathan, the police state. We cannot lay at Hobbes' door everything modern Leviathan has become. Neither can we neglect the fact that three hundred years ago he was its chief architect.

# Suggestions for Discussion and Study

1.  Hobbes suggests in *Leviathan* (The Second Part, Chapter 20) that not only the civil state but also smaller groups, like the family, are based on a contract between individuals. A newborn child must do everything in its power to survive. Its power, of course, is modest, so it enters a silent contract, pledging obedience to its mother or whoever feeds it. Since the mother is often (though not necessarily) dependent on a husband, the child is indirectly subject to the mother's husband. Whether he is also the child's father is unimportant to Hobbes. Biological parenthood in itself involves no special rights or obligations. Thus, for Hobbes the family is not a unit bound together by blood and solicitude, but by economic power.

Authority resides with the breadwinner. In what ways are Hobbes' views relevant to contemporary considerations of the family?

2. Does the Hobbesian concept of the social contract characterize the ways individuals deal with one another in marriage, friendship, business? Does it characterize the ways governments deal with one another in international diplomacy? Cite examples where the social contract is in force.

3. One implication of the Hobbesian image of human nature is that humans—unlike bees and ants—are not instinctively social creatures. Strip away the rules of society and the laws of government and our selfish, predatory traits would fully assert themselves, driving us back into the state of nature. Nobel Prize winner William Golding's novel *Lord of the Flies* tells of a group of adolescents who revert to a Hobbesian state of nature. But this novel is only one variation on the theme. Daniel Defoe's *Robinson Crusoe* is another. What literary works or films can you think of that explore this theme? Write your own essay or story. How would persons behave if they reverted to the state of nature as a result of, say, large-scale natural disaster or nuclear war? Your essay or story may indicate you have a basically different understanding of human nature than Hobbes does. How does your understanding compare with his?

4. As Hobbes sees it, good and evil are relative: that which pleases one person may not please another. Consequently, there can be no absolute good or evil. Both depend upon the person's situation at the time, and as he or she changes, good things may become evil and evil things good. Discuss the Hobbesian notion of good and evil. In offering it, he broke with a long tradition of both Platonic and Christian morality, which point to an absolute, permanent standard of morality in the Good or in God. The debate between Hobbesian relativists and Platonic/Christian absolutists is going on today, assuming various forms. What are some of these forms?

5. Hobbes is a complex thinker who is difficult to pin down because he says contradictory things. For examples: the human being is a rational creature, yet the human being is an irrational creature; individuals are free to express personal desires, yet they are not free, because this very expression leads to personal destruction; the sovereign has absolute authority,

yet not even the sovereign can supplant the individual's right
to self-defense; good and evil are relative to the person, yet the
sovereign, or the state, has the final word on what constitutes
good and evil. Needless to say, Hobbes' seemingly opposing
claims can frustrate the reader. Choose one of these opposing
claims in Hobbes' thought and see if you can reconcile it. Keep
in mind that his grand symbol for the way things work and
interrelate in the universe is the machine. A machine is a whole
made up of parts. Often these parts work in opposition to one
another. Could it be, in spite of contradictions, that Hobbes is
systematic and consistent in the expression of his views?

6. Hobbes is one of the eminent figures of English literature, a
master of English prose style. But this is an aspect of his work
that often gets lost among his critics. One critic who addresses
the literary aspect of Hobbes is R. L. Brett ("Thomas Hobbes,"
in *The English Mind: Studies in the English Moralists presented to
Basil Willey* [Cambridge: At the University Press, 1964], pp.
30–54). Undertake a study of Hobbes, thinking of him as a man
of letters.

# Further Reading

Peters, Richard. *Hobbes*. Baltimore: Penguin, Peregrine Books, 1967. One
of the best modern studies of Hobbes in terms of its readability and
comprehensiveness.

Rogow, Arnold A. *Thomas Hobbes: Radical in the Service of Reaction*. New
York: W. W. Norton & Co., 1986. A scholarly, biographical study
that places Hobbes against the background of his age. Reveals
several facets of Hobbes as a man of letters.

Strauss, Leo. *The Political Philosophy of Hobbes: Its Basis and Its Genesis*.
Chicago: The University of Chicago Press, 1959. A political
philosopher's assessment, which claims that the concepts of vanity
and fear, not the concept of a mechanical universe that he inherited
from Galileo, are at the root of Hobbes' political thought. For
Strauss, Hobbes was and always remained a humanist, in spite of
his pretensions toward science.

Watkins, J. W. N. *Hobbes's System of Ideas: A Study in the Political
Significance of Philosophical Theories*. London: Hutchinson
University Library, 1973. Presents an overview of contemporary

scholarship on Hobbes, while simultaneously indicating the author's view of what Hobbes means to our time.

# Notes

1. Giovanni Pico Della Mirandola, "Oration on the Dignity of Man," trans. Elizabeth Livermore Forbes, in *The Renaissance Philosophy of Man*, eds. Ernst Cassirer, Paul Oskar Kristeller, John Herman Randall Jr. (Chicago: The University of Chicago Press, Phoenix Books, 1948), p. 225.
2. As quoted in *The Metaphysical System of Hobbes*, selected by M. W. Calkins (La Salle, IL: The Open Court Publishing Co., 1963), p. vii.
3. John Aubrey, *Aubrey's Brief Lives*, ed. Oliver Lawson Dick (London: Secker and Warburg, 1950), p. 150.
4. Thomas Hobbes, *Leviathan: Or the Matter, Forme and Power of a Commonwealth Ecclesiastical and Civil*, ed. Michael Oakeshott, sel. Richard S. Peters (New York: Collier Macmillan Publishers, Collier Books, 1962), Author's Introduction, p. 19. (All references to *Leviathan* are to this edition.)
5. Ibid., The First Part, Chapter 2, p. 23.
6. Ibid., p. 24.
7. Ibid., p. 21.
8. Ibid., Chapter 3, p. 35.
9. Ibid., Chapter 4, p. 34.
10. Ibid., Chapter 5, p. 41.
11. Ibid.
12. Ibid., Chapter 4, pp. 36–37.
13. Ibid., p. 39.
14. Ibid., p. 40.
15. Ibid., Chapter 6, pp. 47–48.
16. Ibid., Chapter 13, p. 99.
17. Ibid., p. 101.
18. Ibid., p. 100.
19. Ibid.
20. Ibid., Chapter 14, p. 106.
21. Ibid., Chapter 15, p. 122.
22. Ibid., The Second Part, Chapter 17, p. 132.
23. Thomas Hobbes, *English Works of Thomas Hobbes*, vol. 4, *Human Nature*, ed. William Molesworth (London: John Bohn, 1839–1845; reprint, Darmstadt: Scientia Verlag Aalen, 1966), 33.

# ·5·

# DAVID HUME
## and the image of
# SYMPATHY

# Cultural Background

The Renaissance brought great changes to the intellectual climate of Europe. The discoveries made in astronomy and physics not only revolutionized those sciences but also generated widespread confidence that the mathematical reasoning on which they were based was the key to unlock the secrets of the universe.

Eight years after Hobbes' death, Sir Isaac Newton (1642–1727) published his *Mathematical Principles of Natural Philosophy (1687)*. Newton made fundamental scientific discoveries in the areas of optics, light, gravitation, and mathematics. Building on the work of Galileo and others, he convincingly offered mathematical verification that physical nature behaves according to fixed, definite laws. Here, then, was a definitive vision of the universe as a great mechanical work, which can be known directly by human intellect without the intervention and intermediation of theological or other traditional philosophical authorities.

The task of drawing out the human implications of the Newtonian universe fell variously to thinkers of the eighteenth century, recognized in Western history as the Enlightenment. The term *Enlightenment* denotes not only a historical period but also the philosophical outlook that dominated this period. Having derived from Newton the notion that the ways of the universe are penetrable, Enlightenment thinkers became convinced that human beings, as a part of nature, ultimately can understand everything in their experience, just as they can understand a mathematical or mechanical problem.

A term that is virtually synonymous with the Enlightenment is *optimism*. Enlightenment thinkers were disposed to seeing things from the most promising and hopeful perspectives. They were inspired by a vision of progress and led by a belief that by applying logical, objective thought (reason), humankind could be emancipated from age-old artificialities, restrictions, injustices, and superstitions. The dream of the Enlightenment, says the historian Carl Becker, was to create a religion of humanity, a "Heavenly City"[1] on earth.

That Enlightenment dream proved illusory in its own time, nor has it been realized since. Nonetheless, the eighteenth century contributed in major ways to cultural expansion and social change. Industrial and agricultural progress produced such inventions as the steam engine, the cast-iron bridge, the power loom, the cotton gin. Advances were made in the study of medicine, anthropology, philology, geography, cartography. There were demands for popular education, prison reforms, and the abolition of the slave trade. The American Revolution occurred, which served as a model for the French Revolution and fanned the spirit of democracy around the world.

Religion figured prominently in the life of the period, serving mainly as a battleground for wars of the intellect. Some of the most luminous thinkers of the Enlightenment were decidedly critical of the religious establishment. Voltaire (1694–1778) vilified church-men for identifying with a regressive political and social order. The demand to set religious thought free from old restraints mani-fested itself in new trends: the study of comparative religions; the intense questioning of the historical accuracy of the Bible; the fascination with "noble savages," who were thought to live quite happily without creeds or clergy.

In a scholarly cultural essay, the modern theologian Karl Barth capsulizes the intellectual essence of the Enlightenment as follows:

> Man, who discovers his own power and ability, the poten-tiality dormant in his humanity, that is, his human being as such, and looks upon it as the final, the real and absolute, I mean as something 'detached', self-justifying, with its own authority and power, which he can therefore set in motion in all directions and without any restraint—this is absolute man. … This absolute man is eighteenth-century man, who appears to us more or less distinctly, more or less open or veiled in conventional drapings, in all the human faces of that century which are so different amongst themselves.[2]

Barth suggests that in spite of the many shifts and turns thought took during the Enlightenment, one conception of hu-man nature, that of "absolute man," stood at the center. David Hume was one of the main shapers of this conception.

## Biography

David Hume was born in Edinburgh, Scotland, in 1711 and died there in 1776. Since the sixteenth century, his family had owned a small estate at Ninewells, near the border of England. This is where Hume was reared and where he returned periodically throughout his life. When he was only two years old, his father died, "Leaving me," as the philosopher tells us in his short autobiography, "with an elder Brother and Sister, under the care of our Mother, a woman of singular Merit, who, though young and handsome, devoted herself entirely to the rearing and educating of her children."[3]

Until he was twelve years old, Hume was educated at home. Then he was sent to the University of Edinburgh, where he remained for two or three years, majoring in the classics. From the age of fifteen until he was twenty-three, he lived at Ninewells, studying on his own, developing his literary and philosophical interests. Although his father's estate provided him with a modest annual allowance, the family was far from wealthy, and the question of a career became a pressing one. "My studious disposition, my sobriety, and my industry," he tells us, "gave my family a notion that the law was a proper profession for me; but I found an unsurmountable aversion for everything but the pursuits of philosophy; and while they fancied I was poring over Voet and Vinnius, Cicero and Virgil were the authors I was secretly devouring."[4]

In 1734, Hume left Scotland to work in Bristol, England, as a clerk in a business firm. Deciding after a few months that this was unsuitable work for him, and having so little money, he went to France with the idea of taking up residence in some country retreat where he could live sparsely, maintain his independence, and concentrate on improving his literary and philosophical skills.

The next three years in France were intellectually rigorous and productive ones for Hume. While living first in the city of Rheims and then in the small town of La Flèche in Anjou, he wrote his major philosophical work, *A Treatise of Human Nature*. Only with considerable difficulty did he manage to get the *Treatise* published in England, with the first two volumes appearing in 1739 and the third in 1740. Hume had hoped to gain literary fame and financial success with the publication of this work, but practically everything connected with its appearance proved a disappointment. "Never literary attempt was more unfortunate," he writes, "than my Treatise of Human Nature. It fell *deadborn from the press*, without reaching such distinction, as even to excite a murmur among the zealots."[5]

Hume soon recovered from the setback and proceeded with his scholarly endeavors. With the writing of the *Treatise*, he had set his course as a philosopher, but philosophy was not so sharply separated from other disciplines in the eighteenth century as it is in our day. Philosophers habitually combined philosophical studies with other intellectual pursuits, and Hume was increasingly turning his thoughts to political and historical subjects. In 1741, his *Essays, Moral and Political* appeared. Slowly scholars began to notice him, and when a vacancy for a professor of moral philosophy occurred at the University of Edinburgh, he applied for the position. He then realized that his *Treatise on Human Nature* had made a deeper impact than he had earlier imagined. The conservative professors would not associate with the author of what they regarded as a radical work, and he was promptly turned down for the position. (He was similarly to be refused a position on the faculty of Glasgow University in 1752.)

Since the doors of university teaching were closed to him, and he was in need of employment, Hume became a tutor in 1745 to an unbalanced young nobleman, the Marquis of Annadale, who lived near London. In the following year, Hume left this unsatisfactory post to become secretary to General St. Clair, who took him first to the coast of France on a minor military expedition and then to Austria and Italy as a member of a military embassy. At the end of two years, Hume had accumulated enough money to begin to feel financially stable.

He was now in his late thirties and still craving the literary notoriety that had eluded him. In 1748 he published *An Enquiry Concerning Human Understanding*, which represented a rewriting of many of the basic ideas of his *Treatise*, and *Three Essays, Moral and Political* (1748), which was the first of Hume's books to appear under his own name. Upon returning to his native Scotland in 1749, he set to work for the next few years creating that body of writing which would make him both wealthy and famous.

In 1751 he published *An Enquiry Concerning the Principles of Morals*, which Hume regarded as his "best" book, and the next year *Political Discourses*, the only one of his books "that was successful on the first publication."[6] In 1752 he became librarian of the Advocates Library in Edinburgh. Though it paid little, this position gave him immediate access to a library where he could pursue his study of history. His *History of England* appeared in six volumes between 1754 and 1762. In these volumes, Hume rendered a social and cultural interpretation of historical facts and explained the basic purposes and motives that shape the development of humanity.

During these productive years, when Hume was in his forties and early fifties, he solidified his religious views in two works: *Four Dissertations* (1757), which included the essay "The Natural History of Religion," as well as "Of the Passions," "Of Tragedy," and "The Standard of Taste," and *Dialogues Concerning Natural Religion*. A number of his readers had already taken offense at his views on religion, and rather than make matters worse, he decided not to publish *Dialogues Concerning Natural Religion* during his lifetime. It appeared in 1779, three years after his death.

When Hume had returned to his beloved Scotland in 1749, he had no ambition to live elsewhere again. Nevertheless, at the urging of others, he became secretary to the British Embassy in Paris in 1763. Here he fascinated French society with his ideas and became something of a celebrity at the French court. He interacted with the outstanding French thinkers of the Enlightenment, especially the mathematician Jean D'Alembert (1717–1783) and the philosopher Denis Diderot (1713–1784). He formed a friendship with the philosopher Jean-Jacques Rousseau (1712–1778), which ended in a publicized quarrel between the two men.

He returned to Edinburgh in 1766, where he was to live for the rest of his life. In 1767 he became an Under-Secretary of State, only to retire two years later. By now, Hume was recognized as one of the foremost intellectuals of his time. He spent the last years of his life mainly enjoying the company of friends and entertaining numerous famous guests who came to pay him homage.

Hume's health began to fail in the spring of 1775, and discovering that his disease was terminal, he wrote his short autobiography. The final paragraph of this composition reads:

> To conclude historically with my own character. I am, or rather was (for that is the style I must now use in speaking of myself, which emboldens me the more to speak my sentiments); I was, I say, a man of mild dispositions, of command of temper, of an open, social, and cheerful humour, capable of attachment, but little susceptible of enmity, and of great moderation in all my passions. Even my love of literary fame, my ruling passion, never soured my temper, notwithstanding my frequent disappoint-

ments. My company was not unacceptable to the young and careless, as well as to the studious and literary; and as I took a particular pleasure in the company of modest women, I had no reason to be displeased with the reception I met with from them. In a word, though most men any wise eminent have found reason to complain of calumny, I never was touched or even attacked by her baleful tooth: and though I wantonly exposed myself to the rage of both civil and religious factions, they seemed to be disarmed in my behalf of their wonted fury. My friends never had occasion to vindicate any one circumstance of my character and conduct: not but that the zealots, we may well suppose, would have been glad to invent and propagate any story to my disadvantage, but they could never find any which they thought would wear the face of probability. I cannot say there is no vanity in making this funeral oration of myself, but I hope it is not a misplaced one; and this is a matter of fact which is easily cleared and ascertained.[7]

These are the words of a man who was confident he had lived his life studiously, honestly, congenially, and usefully. Scholarship on Hume over the years has neither added to nor detracted from his own assessment of his character.

# Hume on What Can I Know?

Though Hume lived during the eighteenth century, he was an intellectual heir of the seventeenth. As in the humanism of the Renaissance, the physical and experimental sciences preoccupied thinkers of the seventeenth century. Newton's achievement was the model for all aspiring intellects. Corresponding to the humanists of the Renaissance were numbers of seventeenth-century virtuosi, people who were experimenters and investigators in the arts and sciences. And, as with the humanists of the Renaissance, most of these virtuosi saw their work as serving the cause of religion.

For the virtuosi, God was the guarantor and the goal of physical science. Science would answer the questions philosophy and theology had thus far failed to solve with certainty. Study of the biblical Word of God had occasioned bitter religious differen-ces, intolerance, bloodshed. It was consoling and promising, there-fore, to turn to the physical Works of God. Would not the study of the universe afford another approach to God, just as valid as the biblical Word and far less disputable? The virtuosi were supremely confident in reason (a confidence Hobbes had tried to inspire) and the rationality and handicraft of the divine Architect. The result of this rationalism, however, was that Christianity became a religion of the head rather than the heart. As leading authority Richard Westfall sums it up, "in arguing religion as though it were natural philosophy," the virtuosi in effect challenged Christianity while believing they were arguing on its behalf.[8]

Nevertheless, the virtuosi introduced new attitudes, new standards, and new methods, and their work helped create the intellectual climate of Hume's century. The concept of reason itself underwent an important shift of character in the eighteenth cen-tury. The great European rationalist philosophers of the seven-teenth century—René Descartes (1596–1650) Gottfried Wilhelm Leibniz (1646–1716), Benedict Spinoza (1632–1677)—had reasoned synthetically, creating systems of truth from first principles, argu-ing from axioms to the necessary conclusions of these axioms. Under the influence of John Locke (1632–1704) and George Berkeley (1685–1753) in Britain, however, the concept of reason in the eighteenth century took on a more practical character. No longer was reason basically a systemization of ideas built on axioms; instead, it was an analytic activity of research, a method of testing and doubting, dedicated to discovering the system of nature, including humanity, piecemeal. Everything was open to this analytic reason, not least Christianity and every other received opinion and established institution.

With Hume comes a new phase in Enlightenment thought. The European rationalists and the British empiricists (as Locke and Berkeley are classified) all had something in common, regardless of how they understood reason. They shared a basic confidence in the power of reason to penetrate the manifold mysteries of both physical and human nature. But Hume's investigations into the theory of knowledge led him to the conviction that any great confidence in the power of reason was a misplaced confidence. Hume, who is also often classified as an empiricist, marks that phase in Enlightenment thought where it was beginning to ques-tion the rational basis of its own optimism.

Hume's theory of knowledge presupposes severe limits to what we can know. He develops his theory in Book I of *A Treatise of Human Nature* and again in his *Enquiry Concerning Human Understanding*. He calls the content of the mind *perceptions* and divides perceptions into two classes: *impressions* and *ideas*.[9] Impressions are lively perceptions that occur when we touch, see, hear, taste, smell, love, hate, will, desire. Our ideas are copies of impressions; they differ from impressions only in degree, not in kind. We will closely approximate Hume's distinction between impressions and ideas if we contrast the smelling of a rose to the thought of smelling a rose. Certainly, the smelling of a rose (impression) is more direct and more vivid than the thought (idea) of smelling it. To trace our ideas back to impressions is to trace them back to the elements of which they are composed. There is no other source of knowledge than impressions.

Some of our ideas are simple and exactly resemble their antecedent impressions, such as the color red, while others are complex and may not resemble anything we've ever had an impression of, such as a red-winged horse. Then how, we might ask, do complex ideas originate? Hume says they come to be through a process of association, whereby simple ideas (red, wing, horse) combine to produce complex ones. This process of association reveals two basic powers of the mind: the power to remember, or record (memory), and the power to imagine, or invent (imagination).

The process of association is automatically at work in us, even in our most idle daydreams. It's the way the mind, by nature, functions. Ideas are associated with a certain regularity and, as Hume perceives, according to three types of relations: *resemblance* (a portrait of a person makes us think of that person), *contiguity* in time and space (the idea of the White House occurs side by side with the idea of Washington, D.C.), and *causation* (rain and wetness).[10]

Hume maintains that not one of these three relations reveals to us any *necessary* connection between our ideas. (The only place he finds necessary connection, or what he calls *relations of ideas*,[11] is in demonstratively certain propositions, as contained in geometry, algebra, and arithmetic). We merely happen to find that when various ideas are associated in any one of these three ways, the thought that ideas are connected rises quite naturally. Of the three types of relations by which we associate ideas, Hume devotes the most attention to the relation of causation.

All of our reasoning about events and objects in the world, or what Hume calls *matters of fact*, is based on the relation of cause and effect. If we watch a piece of ice melt on a hot stove, we immediately infer that the heat of the stove has *caused* the ice to melt. But Hume wants to understand, and wants us to understand, on what grounds we draw such inferences. To this end he offers the following illustration:

> The first time a man saw the communication of motion by impulse, as by the shock of two billiard balls, he could not pronounce that the one event was *connected*: but only that it was *conjoined* with the other. After he has observed several instances of this nature, he then pronounces them to be *connected*. What alteration has happened to give rise to this new idea of *connexion*? Nothing but that he now *feels* these events to be *connected* in his imagination.[12]

We recall that for Hume there is no other source of knowledge than impressions. But from what impression does "connexion" derive? We do not actually witness any power being transferred between the two billiard balls. From a single sequence of billiard balls, we don't know what will follow what. On the basis of repeated experience, or "custom," however, we draw causal inferences, custom for Hume simply being a habit of thought based on repeated experience.[13]

And so it is with all knowledge concerning matters of fact. When we regularly experience D followed by E, we come to anticipate E whenever D appears. This feeling of anticipation leads us to think there's a necessary connection between D and E. But when we closely attend to the situation, Hume insists, we find that D and E are entirely distinct and separate. We have no proof they are connected.

Hume's analysis of causation requires a denial of any objective knowledge about the world. He admits we know the existence of our own ideas, but he insists we are closed in by them. All we can be sure of is a parade of individual ideas, one following the other, in a place called the *mind*. Indeed, he asserts that the mind itself "is nothing but a heap or collection of different perceptions, united together by certain relations, and suppos'd tho' falsely, to be endow'd with a perfect simplicity and identity."[14] Hume claims that we know nothing about the world, and even our perceptions do not add up to a distinct notion of self. His skepticism cuts very deep.

## Hume on What Ought I to Do?

But there's a practical side to Hume's philosophy, as well as this skeptical one. All we can know with any measure of assurance, he says, is what goes on inside us; there is nothing else to depend on. Still, when we examine what does go on inside us, we find that it's virtually impossible to believe that all of the things in the world around us do not really exist. Our acceptance of the external world is instinctive and powerful. For all the rigor of our philosophical arguments, it keeps coming back to us in the raw data of experience. Should we not, then, take experience, rather than reason, as our guide and get on with the practical business of living? In a word, the practical side of Hume's philosophy takes for granted much that the skeptical side rejects, and it's from this practical side that he affirms the general moral structure of Enlightenment society.

A thinker of the ancient Roman world to whom Hume often refers with admiration is Cicero (106–43 B.C.). Cicero and Hume are kindred spirits, in spite of the great span of time that separates them. As one reads Cicero's philosophic writings such as *De Finibus* and *Academica*, one is constantly impressed by the sharpness of his distinctions and by the manner in which he turns philosophical conclusions to practical interests. Shrewdly practical, he's greatly attracted to a theory of knowledge that sees the probable, rather than the certain, as within the reach of the human mind.

In discussing the philosophies of other thinkers, Cicero distrusts positions that would result in the moral structure of society disintegrating. He admires positions that emphasize character, for he sees these as giving a sound basis for the moral life of the individual, the state, and humanity. We discover Cicero's practicality in Hume. For both of these thinkers, the actual problems of human, and especially moral, experience tease the imagination and search the intelligence.

Hume's central question in his moral writings is, What is the essence of morality? Some philosophers, as Philippa Foot points out,

> talk about morality in an elevated tone; and they seem to be entirely sincere, finding virtue a sublime and noble subject, the pursuit of virtue an inspiring life's work. So it is, for instance, with Kant, who writes in one place about the moral law within and the starry heavens above filling the mind with ever increasing awe and admiration, the oftener and more steadily we reflect on them. It came quite naturally to Kant, as it did to Rousseau, to talk about the sublimity of our nature in its higher aspect, and of *reverence* for the moral law. 'Duty!' he says. 'Sublime and mighty name.'[15]

But in Hume's attempts to penetrate the essence of morality, we seldom hear him speak of morality in terms of praise or lofty aspiration. His whole approach to the subject is much more down-to-earth. In a famous passage, he writes:

> And as every quality which is useful or agreeable to ourselves or others is, in common life, allowed to be a part of personal merit; so no other will ever be received, where men judge of things by their natural, unprejudiced reason, without the delusive glosses of superstition and false religion. Celibacy, fasting, penance, mortification, self-denial, humility, silence, solitude, and the whole train of monkish virtues; for what reason are they everywhere rejected by men of sense, but because they serve to no manner of purpose; neither advance a man's fortune in the world, nor render him a more valuable member of society; neither qualify him for entertainment of company, nor increase his power of self-enjoyment? We observe, on the contrary, that they cross all these desirable ends; stupify the understanding and harden the heart, obscure the fancy and sour the temper. We justly, therefore, transfer them to the opposite column, and place them in the catalogue of vices; nor has any superstition force sufficient among men of the world, to pervert entirely these natural sentiments. A gloomy, hair-brained enthusiast, after his death, may

have a place in the calendar; but will scarcely ever be admitted, when alive, into intimacy and society, except by those who are as delirious and dismal as himself.[16]

Any student of composition might find this an excellent passage for analysis. It bristles with ideas, is marked by an acid wit, and is deliberate in its purpose (not to mention that it exemplifies certain logical fallacies such as question-begging and ad hominem). In one sentence, Hume demolishes the whole tradition of "monkish virtues" that had been fostered within Christianity. These virtues have no place in his conception of morality, namely, conduct that is useful. If we ask, Useful to whom? Hume's answer is clear: useful to ourselves and human society at large.

Human beings are equipped, fortunately, to lead useful moral lives. They are universally endowed by nature with the feeling, or sentiment, of *sympathy*. In interpreting this sentiment in Books II and III of the *Treatise* (and again in *An Enquiry Concerning the Principles of Morals*, where he substitutes the term "benevolence" for sympathy), Hume purports to base his conclusions on observation, not on any traditional theory of morality.

When we see another person in distress, for example, the suffering of that person causes us to suffer. The feelings of one person affect the feelings of another. Through the sentiment of sympathy we are able to feel another's pain as our own. This sympathy is naturally aroused in us and causes us to want to help. (Think of pleas on TV and in newspapers on behalf of the helpless, homeless, and starving in distant places.) We want to help, not out of some superimposed sense of duty, but because we have a genuine "fellow-feeling" with the other. When we see someone else helping a person in distress, we are pleased with that person's action.

This pleasure is also an affect of sympathy. We are pleased because the person in distress is being helped and because of the selflessness of the person helping. We are moved by our sympathy to approve of the action of the helper. Human beings are disposed by nature to sympathize with one another. They are also disposed to feel pleasure at the sight of actions that alleviate pain or cause pleasure and to feel pain at the sight of actions that do the opposite. Human beings are moved to approval and disapproval; these feelings alone make the actions they are directed to either virtuous or vicious.

Hume thus offers a strongly anti-intellectual theory of morality. For him, the absence of reasons is the most obvious truth about morality. We do not make moral judgments and perform moral acts on the basis of having arrived at them intellectually; we make these judgments and perform these acts on the basis of sympathy.

If we ask ourselves why we judge a certain kind of conduct to be morally wrong, we'll have to conclude that we do not *think* it wrong, we *feel* it to be wrong. Hume presses this point by asking us to "see if you can find that matter of fact, or real existence, which you call *vice*,"[17] and he argues that in

> which-ever way you take it, you find only certain passions, motives, volitions, and thoughts. There is no other matter of fact in the case. . . . You never can find it, till you turn your reflexion into your own breast, and find a sentiment of disapprobation, which arises in you, toward this action. Here is a matter of fact; but 'tis the object of feeling, not of reason. It lies in yourself, not in the object.[18]

Hume runs the risk of reducing morality to a matter of taste, where moral judgments are subjective and relative. But this risk is perhaps more obvious to us in our age of pluralism than it was to Hume. He holds the general Enlightenment belief that human beings are much alike everywhere. They share the same sentiment of sympathy. "It is needless," he claims, "to push our researches so far as to ask, why we have humanity or a fellow-feeling with others. It is sufficient, that this is experienced to be a principle in human nature."[19] Thus understood, sympathy is a universal sentiment that exists in its own right, quite apart from our ability to account for it. On the basis of sympathy, human beings share the same tastes and make the same judgments. Hume's arguments for sympathy as a universal sentiment cannot be proved either true or false; they are simply an expression of Enlightenment optimism.

Hume's theory of morality differs strikingly from that advanced by Hobbes, though both men focus on the ordinary world of human affairs. Hobbes maintains that life is "solitary, poor, nasty, brutish, and short"[20] and individuals are ruled by fear and self-interest. Hume rejects the Hobbesian notion "that all *benevolence* is mere hypocrisy, friendship a cheat, public spirit a farce, fidelity a snare."[21]

According to him, self-interest does not control human motivation. We are moved, he says, to praise actions performed in distant ages and remote countries, which obviously cannot relate to our self-interest. We are deeply moved by accounts of the goodness or the wickedness of imagined characters in novels and dramas. A bitter enemy may perform a high-minded deed, which elicits our admiration. Far from being a mere pretense in human beings, the natural feeling of kindness may even be observed in animals. Only willful distortion of the facts can deny parental tenderness, selfless devotion, or a thousand other signals of a genuine, general benevolence in human nature. Hume does not judge the degrees of benevolence and self-interest in human nature. He simply recognizes that "some particle of the dove [is] kneaded into our nature, along with elements of the wolf and serpent."[22] A true understanding of morality, he maintains, must duly recognize humanity and friendship. If it merely highlights human self-interest, it's more like a satire than an accurate account of the natural moral disposition of humankind.

Basil Willey hits the mark when he says Hume thinks "well of human nature."[23] Hume is impressed by the place of benevolence and cooperation in all successful life and achievement. We do not put our own pleasures and interests out of sight, he maintains, in genuinely seeking the well-being of others. Individual human life is fulfilled only amid the well-being of society as a whole. The virtues that we promote must benefit and be useful to other persons, as well as ourselves. As a moralist, Hume does not present us with a catalogue of virtues we ought to promote. His thinking contains a strong element of do-as-you-would-be-done-by, which presumes that ordinary human beings know very well the difference between virtue and vice. Willey is again accurate when he says Hume "presents morality to us as attractive rather than imperative, and attractive because it promises us the greatest happiness as the world understands happiness."[24]

# Hume on for What Can I Hope?

After Voltaire, Hume was the most notorious enemy of orthodox religion in Europe. For several nights after his burial, two men were assigned to guard his tomb for fear of its being desecrated. Yet, this same philosopher whose religious views piqued the anger of many was held in high esteem by those who knew him best. Adam Smith (1732–1790), author of *The Wealth of Nations*, was Hume's lifelong friend. Shortly after Hume's death, Smith wrote: "Upon the whole, I have always considered him, both in his lifetime and since his death, as approaching as nearly to the idea of a perfectly wise and virtuous man, as perhaps the nature of human frailty will permit."[25]

James Boswell (1740–1795), journalist and biographer of Dr. Johnson (1709–1784), interviewed Hume in his last days in the hope of recording Hume's deathbed confession concerning his hope for immortality. Not only was Boswell disappointed that such a confession wasn't made, he was baffled by the dying philosopher's calm indifference to the subject. Hume seems to have been a man who, in his old age, had no yearning for certainty beyond the reach of human capacity.[26]

Hume is not so much concerned with the ultimate destiny of the self and humanity as he is with relationships that exist in the here and now between individuals. From a Humian standpoint, human nature is not something that an individual can study and describe as his or her own private possession. This is one of the discoveries Hume makes by intensely probing the question of knowledge. Near the end of Book I of the *Treatise*, having reached the conclusion that he cannot even say what it means to be a self, he cries out:

> Where am I, or what? From what causes do I derive my existence, and to what condition shall I return? Whose favour shall I court, and whose anger must I dread? What beings surround me? and on whom have I any influence, or who have any influence on me?[27]

Hume immediately tells us that he recovers the self only by going among other persons, conversing, playing a game of backgammon, being merry with his friends. Every individual comes to see who and what he or she is through relationships with others. We come to have a self and to know our own nature in that mode of communion Hume calls *sympathy*.

Hume's indifference to the subject of immortality, which troubled Boswell so, can be explained by saying he sees no hope beyond this world. But Hume does see hope within it. What Becker says about the secular philosophers of the eighteenth century as a whole applies emphatically to Hume: "For the love of God they substituted love of humanity; for the vicarious atonement the perfectibility of man through his own efforts; and for the hope of immortality in another world the hope of living in the memory of future generations."[28] Hume's doctrine of sympathy is part and parcel of a sweeping Enlightenment vision, according to which there exists a great commonwealth of humanity. What we can hope for and work toward as individuals is a sympathetic, qualitative life within this commonwealth.

## Implications of the Humian Image of Human Nature

At the core of the Humian image of human nature is the claim that we need not know anything certain about the ultimate ends of life in order to discharge our obligations. Indeed, we do not need to know why we do anything; our emotive capacity picks us up and carries our reason and will along.

If we look at the Humian image from a historical perspective, we can readily see how it conflicts with two major interpretations of human nature in Western thought that preceded it: the Platonic and the Christian. For over two thousand years, from Plato to the period of the Enlightenment, the idea that human beings are rational creatures held a prominent place. Reason was thought to be the most important and distinguishing characteristic of human nature. It could rule a human being's actions, and he or she could therefore be rationally persuaded and perfected by education. Perhaps the greatest educator of all time, Plato believed human beings could be taught to achieve perfection.

Equally important in the development of Western thought, but in partial contrast to the Platonic view, was the Christian view of the human being as a child of God, the creature made in the divine image and endowed with an immortal soul. Though reason was recognized as an important characteristic of human nature and was used to expound Christian thought, it was also suspected of leading to error and arrogance. Through spirituality and faith, rather, human beings would achieve perfection. A common question was Where does humanity's best interest reside? For Platonists, it was in reason; for Christians, it was in God.

Hume denies that either Platonism or Christianity located the true pulse of human nature. The human being is neither a rational creature nor a child of God. For Hume, the human being is a creature of feeling—not just any feeling, but fellow-feeling. This feeling does not require any explanation in theological terms. It belongs to life itself and is that which undergirds and advances all human endeavor.

Hume declares that he is portraying human nature as it actually is. But it's hard to read him long without sensing that his is anything but a neutral description. He's actually offering a *belief* about humanity, and what he believes is that human beings are basically creatures of feeling, that they naturally strive to get along with one another, and that this striving produces the highest form of human happiness.

Since history offers so much evidence of the cruelty of human beings toward one another, we are inclined to wonder if Hume and the whole Enlightenment did not simply look at the world through rose-colored glasses. Our wonder deepens when we consider that both the seventeenth and eighteenth centuries were periods of devastating religious and political strife and bloodshed. Was not the Enlightenment emphasis on human solidarity merely wishful thinking? What credence can we place today in the Humian notion that the human being is a creature of sympathy?

As much credence, perhaps, as we can place in such organizations as the Red Cross and the Peace Corps or as we can place in such international agreements as The United Nations Charter (1945) and the Universal Declaration of Human Rights (1948). If sympathy did not exist among human beings, would such organizations and agreements even exist? A very large element of sympathy does exist in human nature, but whether it is or can be the ruling element are harder questions to answer. Some philosophers think poorly of humanity; others think highly. In our darkened century, Hume serves to remind us to think well of ourselves and to manifest the element of sympathy that is within us.

# Suggestions for Discussion and Study

1. Hume's views on morality differ dramatically from those of Hobbes. In your opinion, is the human being a creature of sympathy or a creature of egoism? Both a creature of sympathy and of egoism? Neither a creature of sympathy nor of egoism? What are your reasons for answering as you do? Notice the *kinds* of reasons you offer. Are they psychological, religious, scientific, economic, political, or philosophical in character? What kinds of reasons does Hume offer?

2. Basil Willey writes: "Before [Hume], Nature and Reason go hand in hand; after him, Nature and Feeling. Hume was 'indispensable', if only because, by the very completeness of his destructive efficacy, he showed that man cannot live by Reason alone" (*The Eighteenth Century Background: Studies on the Idea of Nature in the Thought of the Period* [New York: Columbia University Press, 1965], p. 111). According to Hume, why can human beings not live by reason alone? The Romantic movement came upon the heels of the Enlightenment. How does Hume contribute to Romanticism?

3. "Nature" is a murky term. Go to the *Oxford English Dictionary* and look it up. Hume uses it in at least two basic senses: to refer to things outside us and to things inside us. Yet, he says, we can know only things within us. *Solipsism* is the doctrine that no reality exists other than one's self; the self (mind, consciousness) constitutes the totality of existence. Is Hume a solipsist? Why or why not?

4. In a famous passage, Hume raises an important question about the basis of moral obligation. The passage goes like this:

In every system of morality, which I have hitherto met with, I have always remark'd, that the author proceeds for some time in the ordinary way of reasoning, and establishes the being of a God, or makes observations concerning human affairs; when of a sudden I am surpriz'd to find, that instead of the usual copulations of propositions, *is*, and *is not*, I meet with no proposition that is not connected with an *ought*, or an *ought not*. This change is imperceptible; but is, however, of the last consequence. For as this *ought*, or *ought not*, expresses some new relation or affirmation, 'tis necessary that it shou'd be observ'd and explain'd; and at the same time that a reason should be given, for what seems altogether inconceivable, how this new relation can be a deduction from others, which are entirely different from it (*Treatise*, Book III, Part I, Section I, p. 469).

Let's briefly illustrate what Hume means in this passage. If I should say, "Emma and Bill have been going steady for five years; they say they love one another," I'm making factual assertions. But then I go on to say, "Emma and Bill ought to get married." When I introduce *ought* into my remarks, I'm no longer simply making factual assertions; I'm suggesting that Emma and Bill have a moral obligation to get married. Hume is asking how we can derive *ought* from *is*. How can facts impose obligations on us? If Hume is right—that we cannot derive ought from is—where does our sense of moral obligation come from? Here are three possibilities: the ought is self-imposed; the ought is socially imposed; the ought is divinely imposed. Which of these possibilities comes closest to representing the sense of moral obligation in Hume? Which of them comes closest to representing your sense of moral obligation?

5. Hume indicates that when we look within ourselves, all we find there are "impressions." He also indicates that passions, or feelings, always attend our impressions. Try it out for yourself. Shut your eyes, think of a specific color, like red, and picture objects you associate with it—apples, blood, stop signs, shoes, red anything. Do your impressions of these objects arouse feelings? What kind of feelings? Make a list of these objects and try to define the feelings each of them arouses in you. Is there any pattern to your feelings? Do the same with objects you associate with a different color, like blue—flowers, water, skies, birds, cars, boats, blue anything. Again, is there any pattern to your feelings? Apart from giving a glimpse into the incredible intertwining of memory, imagination, and sense experience, this exercise indicates the kind of thinking Hume does when he tries to plumb the mysteries of that thing we are in the habit of calling the mind.

6. Even the tough-minded Hume was troubled by the fact that the self did not seem to exist. Hovering always in the background of the question of the self is the question of immor-

tality. Some persons believe in immortality; some do not. What difference does it make in our lives here and now whether we do or do not believe in immortality? Write an essay on this subject. A point of departure might be the modern Spanish thinker Miguel de Unamuno's *Tragic Sense of Life*, wherein he argues that without a hunger for immortality, the life of the individual is significantly impoverished.

# Further Reading

Berlin, Isaiah, ed. *The Age of Enlightenment: The 18th Century Philosophers.* New York. The New American Library, A Mentor Book, 1956. Presents basic writings of Locke, Voltaire, Berkeley, Hume, and others with helpful introductions by Berlin.

Gay, Peter. *The Enlightenment: An Interpretation, The Rise of Modern Paganism.* New York: Random House, Vintage Books, 1968. An in-depth study of intellectual history.

Hampson, Norman. *The Enlightenment: An Evaluation of Its Assumptions, Attitudes and Values.* New York: Penguin Books, 1984. Suggests there is a cluster of characteristic attitudes which, when they occur in high enough concentration, we call the Enlightenment. Easy to read.

Humphreys, A. R. *The Augustan World: Society, Thought and Letters in Eighteenth-Century England.* New York: Harper Torchbooks, 1963. Compresses the whole field of life and letters in eighteenth-century England and shows Hume in a broad cultural light.

Livingston, Donald W. *Hume's Philosophy of Common Life.* Chicago: University of Chicago Press, 1985. A comprehensive interpretation of Hume's philosophy based on all of his writings, historical as well as philosophical.

Mossner, Ernest Campbell. *The Life of David Hume*, 2nd ed. Oxford: Oxford University Press, 1980. The most authoritative biography of Hume available.

Smith, Norman Kemp. *The Philosophy of David Hume: A Critical Study of Its Origins and Central Doctrines.* New York: St. Martin's Press, 1966. The touchstone of many interpretations of Hume's philosophy.

# Notes

1. Carl Becker, *The Heavenly City of the Philosophers* (New Haven, CT: Yale University Press, 1952), p. 31.
2. Karl Barth, *Protestant Thought: From Rousseau to Ritschl* (New York: Harper & Row, Publishers, 1959), pp. 14–15.
3. "The Life of David Hume, Esq., Written by Himself," in *David Hume: Essays Moral, Political, and Literary*, ed. Eugene F. Miller, rev. ed. (Indianapolis: Liberty Classics, 1987), p. xxxii. (All quotations from Hume's autobiography are from this edition.)
4. Ibid., p. xxxiii.
5. Ibid., p. xxxiv.
6. Ibid., p. xxxvi.
7. Ibid., pp. xl–xli.
8. Richard S. Westfall, *Science and Religion in Seventeenth Century England* (New Haven, CT: Yale University Press, 1958), p. 141.
9. David Hume, *A Treatise of Human Nature*, ed. L. Al Selby-Bigge. 2nd ed. with text revised and notes by P. H. Nidditch (Oxford: Oxford University Press, 1985), Book I, Part I, Section I, p. 1. (All quotations from Hume's *Treatise* are from this edition.)
10. Ibid., Part III, Section VI, pp. 92–93.
11. David Hume, *An Enquiry Concerning Human Understanding*, in *Enquiries Concerning the Human Understanding and Concerning the Principles of Morals*, ed. L. A. Selby-Bigge, 2nd ed. (Oxford: Oxford University Press, 1972), Section IV, Part II, p. 35. (All quotations from Hume's *An Enquiry Concerning Human Understanding* and from his *An Enquiry Concerning the Principles of Morals* are from this edition.)
12. Ibid., Section VII. Part II, pp. 75–76.
13. Hume, *Treatise*, op. cit., Book I, Part III, Section VIII, pp. 104–105.
14. Ibid., Part IV, Section II, p. 207.
15. Phillipa Foot, *Virtues and Vices and Other Essays in Moral Philosophy* (Berkeley: University of California Press, 1978), p. 74.
16. Hume, *An Enquiry Concerning the Principles of Morals*, op. cit., Section IX, Part I, p. 270.
17. Hume, *Treatise*, op. cit., Book III, Part I, Section I, p. 468.
18. Ibid., pp. 468–469.
19. Hume, *An Enquiry Concerning the Principles of Morals*, op. cit., footnote to Section V, Part II, p. 219.
20. Thomas Hobbes, *Leviathan*, ed. Michael Oakeshott, sel. Richard S. Peters (New York: Collier Macmillan Publishers, Collier Books, 1962), The First Part, Chapter 13, p. 100.
21. Hume, *An Enquiry Concerning the Principles of Morals*, op. cit., Appendix II, p. 295.
22. Ibid., Section IX, Part I, p. 271.
23. Basil Willey, *The English Moralists* (New York: W. W. Norton & Co., Inc., 1964), p. 256.
24. Ibid., p. 259.
25. Adam Smith, "Letter from Adam Smith," in *David Hume: Essays*, op. cit., p. xlix.

26. Ernest Campbell Mossner, *The Life of David Hume*, 2nd ed. (Oxford: Oxford University Press, 1980), p. 588.
27. Hume, *Treatise*, op. cit., Book I, Part IV, Section VII, p. 269.
28. Becker, op. cit., p. 130.

# ·6·

# JOHN DEWEY
# and the image of
# CHANGE

# Cultural Background

If in the development of astronomy and physics it was ultimately Newton who displaced the earth from the center of the universe, then in the development of biology it was ultimately Darwin who displaced the human being from the center of the earth. Darwin's work effectively took human life off of a pedestal and placed it on a level with all other life. Darwin explained nature as a temporal flux in which life undergoes change very slowly. According to his theory of biological evolution, the whole of life is subject to change and will eventually be reduced to nothingness in the gnawing teeth of time.

Darwin's theory of evolution, which we described in the Introduction, found many philosophical counterparts soon after it was formulated. Thinkers immediately saw that Darwin's conclusions had the most far reaching implications for traditional ways of thinking about human nature. Contrary to what Christian tradition had taught, for instance, human beings were not the unique product of a special creative act of God, nor were they made in God's image. Instead, they had emerged through an aimless process of selection from a line of ancestors that led back to some unknown, elemental beginning. What became, then, of the familiar aspirations and hopes, of the settled Christian ideals and foundation of moral principles?

The application of Darwin's theory was frankly adopted by Friedrich Nietzsche (1844–1900) and consistently carried through in his writings on morality. He held that living beings have a "Will to Power,"[1] a desire to dominate, and that since this urge is natural and fundamental, it is "Beyond Good and Evil."[2] In accord with nature, the strong (the masters) ought to have their way in total disregard of the weak (the slaves). Out of these superior masters a higher form of being will, in time, evolve—the "*Superman*."[3] Nietzsche's model for the master class is "the blond beast,"[4] the lion-hearted personality who rules by strength. For Nietzsche, the Christian virtues of love and humility were signs of a degenerate morality. Might makes right. Hitler and his followers pursued Nietzschean morality with notorious results.

But the influence of Darwin upon philosophers who came after him took at least two different directions. In Nietzsche it became a belief in a ruthless, individual will to power; in other thinkers, such as Thomas Huxley (1825–1895) and Herbert Spencer (1820–1903), it became a belief in the development of social instincts in successive generations of the race. These thinkers represented what might be called a *moderate*, as opposed to a *radical*, moral version of Darwin's theory of evolution.

Among the moderate Darwinians on American soil were William James (1842–1910) and John Dewey (1859–1952). James is usually regarded as the founder of the philosophic movement called *pragmatism*, though his friend, Charles Sanders Peirce (1839–1914) anticipated James in using the term to describe a particular philosophical stance.

Pragmatism (which Dewey preferred to call *instrumentalism*) provided a philosophical justification for the human pursuit of practical activities within a world that was steadily progressing along scientific and technological lines. To view life pragmatically is to view it in terms of the next specific problem that has to be solved, not in terms of some far-off ideals or goals that supposedly will result in ultimate human perfection or happiness.

The human being, according to the pragmatic stance, is a thinker and a doer whose thinking and doing are generated out of immediate necessity. There is little space in life for idle speculation. The passwords of pragmatism are "keep moving," "be on guard," "choose carefully where you walk." Life is not so much to be contemplated—asking abstruse questions of whence and whither—as to be improved piece by piece, situation by situation, with whatever resources are at our command. By no accident, pragmatism took root and flourished in the growing technological and industrial society of late nineteenth- and early twentieth-century America. Nor did it accidentally encapsulate and foster those human traits that are widely regarded today as typically American. It stresses the practical use of intelligence, persistent work, and decisive action as the keys to success in the struggle for existence.

# Biography

John Dewey was born in the town of Burlington, Vermont, in 1859, the same year that Darwin's *Origin of the Species* was published. He came from a long line of New England farmers and tradesmen. His father, who had abandoned farming to become a grocer, loved to recite Shakespeare and Milton. His mother, who was a deeply pious woman, insisted that her three sons attend Sunday school, church services, and properly observe the Sabbath in other ways.

Dewey attended the public schools of Burlington and then went on to the University of Vermont, where he prepared to become a teacher. For two-and-a-half years after completing undergraduate studies, Dewey taught high school; first in Oil City, Pennsylvania, and then in Charlotte, Vermont. But in the fall of 1882, he entered Johns Hopkins University in Baltimore, for advanced study in philosophy. A diligent worker, Dewey applied himself with such intensity that he completed his Doctor's degree in philosophy in just two years.

Dewey served on the faculty of several universities during his career: ten years at the University of Michigan; one year at the University of Minnesota; ten years at The University of Chicago; and twenty-five years, until his retirement in 1929, at Columbia University in New York City. In the course of his career, Dewey traveled and lectured in countries around the globe, making an especially profound impression in China. Upon his retirement, he continued to study and write on a range of subjects and to work for numerous political and humanitarian causes. At the time of his death in 1952, at age ninety-two, he was widely acknowledged as America's greatest living philosopher.

It's hard to imagine the rapid changes modern civilization underwent in Dewey's lifetime. He was born the year before Abraham Lincoln became President of the United States and died the year Dwight D. Eisenhower became President. In those nine decades, he saw the inventions of the light bulb, the automobile, and the airplane; he was witness to two world wars, the detonation of the atomic bomb, the rise of communism in the world, and the division of world political influence between the Union of Soviet Socialist Republics and the United States of America. Never content to confine himself simply to technical matters of philosophy, Dewey pondered the changes civilization was undergoing and asked himself what educational skills were required to meet the demands of modern life. No matter where we approach Dewey in the vast body of his work, we always discover his urgent concern for education.

During his years at The University of Chicago (1894–1904), Dewey was chairman of the Department of Philosophy, Psychology, and Pedagogy. This position enabled him to establish the famous Laboratory School in Chicago (1896). With the assistance of his wife, Harriet Alice Chipman, Dewey conducted an educational experiment that involved ideals of learning by doing. Whereas traditional education had tried to instill obedience and receptivity, he tried to cultivate activity, initiative, diversity, and democratic, or voluntary, cooperation. His writings on education during these years, notably *The School and Society* (1899) and *The Child and the Curriculum* (1902), crystallized in his famous *Democracy and Education* (1916). Dewey's ideals brought about a revolution that continues to affect educational theory and practice today.

Dewey's productivity as a writer increased with his move to Columbia University in 1904. (A bibliographical listing of his articles in professional journals and periodicals and his books covers dozens of pages.) But there is also a deep familial side to Dewey the scholar. He and his wife had six children, three boys and three girls. Two of the boys died in early childhood. Later, when traveling in Italy, the Deweys adopted an Italian boy.

In 1927, Dewey's first wife died, leaving a great void in his life. After her death, he shared an apartment with one or another of his children before remarrying in 1946 at age eighty-seven. His second wife, Roberta Lowitz Grant, was forty-two at the time of their marriage. They adopted two Belgian children, a sister and a brother orphaned in the Second World War.

Dewey was slight of build, somewhat halting in speech, and reserved in manner. His outward appearance belied his authorship of such monumental philosophical works as *Reconstruction in Philosophy* (1920), *Human Nature and Conduct* (1922), *Experience and Nature* (1925), *The Quest for Certainty* (1929), and *Art as Experience* (1934). His work as a whole has placed him in the forefront of modern thinkers who have broadly interpreted the discipline of philosophy and applied it to practical problems of human existence.

# Dewey on
# What Can I Know?

Dewey is a sprawling thinker who develops his ideas from one work to the other, always staying within a pragmatic, or instrumentalist, frame of reference. Although no single work gives us all of Dewey's ideas, we can do no better than turn to *The School and Society* if we want to go quickly to the heart of his thought. For example, nowhere does he more sharply outline his image of human nature than in the following passage:

> The activities of life are of necessity directed to bringing the materials and forces of nature under the control of our purposes; of making them tributary to ends of life. Men have had to work in order to live. In and through their work they have mastered nature, they have protected and enriched the conditions of their own life, they have been awakened to the sense of their own powers—have been led to invent, to plan, and to rejoice in the acquisition of skill. In a rough way, all occupations may be classified as gathering about man's fundamental relations to the world in which he lives through getting food to maintain life; securing clothing and shelter to protect and ornament it, and thus, finally, to provide a permanent home in which all the higher and more spiritual interests may center. It is hardly unreasonable to suppose that interests which have such a history behind them must be of the worthy sort.[5]

In this passage, Dewey depicts the human being as a creature whose thinking and doing are generated out of the necessity for competing with nature, or environment, in order to live. As human beings we are exceeded by other creatures in keenness of eyesight, sense of smell, and the ability to distinguish sounds. We are poorly adapted for survival, particularly in our lack of a hairy covering to protect us from the elements and by our long period of dependency, during which we burden our parents until we can be self-sustaining. We are not well equipped, compared with some other creatures, in size, strength, and speed; we have no wings, fins, teeth or claws. Yet in spite of our biological limitations, we possess an intelligence that is manifestly superior to that of all other creatures. Our problem-solving, or *reflective*, intelligence, according to Dewey, allows us to deal successfully with our environment and to become in large measure its masters.

Thinking, of course, leads to the establishment of specific knowledge, but Dewey is more concerned with the activity of thought than with any specific knowledge to which it might lead. In *Quest for Certainty*, he invites us to consider his view of thinking in comparison with views from the past. The proper aim of thinking, he declares, is (1) not to discover abstract forms laid out in nature (Aristotle); (2) not to recognize something behind nature that caused and sustains it (Augustine); and (3) not to discern the mechanistic laws of nature (Hobbes).

Thinking, Dewey insists, is not a quest for "certainty," as though it were possible to acquire knowledge of a static, eternal quality in things. Thinking, rather, is the act of trying to achieve an adjustment between ourselves and our environment, which is always changing and in which we, as biological organisms, are also always changing. There's simply no way to gain a spectator's vantage point on life. In Dewey's opinion, our thinking is not separate from, but a part of, nature and continuous with it. As creatures, we are wholly immersed in life, which means that what we think about and have knowledge of never exceeds our experience of life.

More than most modern philosophers, Dewey addresses the practical question of how human beings can improve upon their ability to think, and this concern leads him to place great importance on the concept of education. The central task of education in the schools is not to press upon persons a given curriculum; its main task, rather, is to enable persons to develop those native powers of observation, experimentation, and reflection that are critical for dealing with the concrete problems of life. He is emphatic that education should not be construed as ending with a certain number of years of formal instruction. Education, Dewey insists, must continue as long as one lives. Schools ought to make their pupils "capable of further education: more sensitive to conditions of growth and more able to take advantage of them. Acquisition of skill, possession of knowledge, attainment of culture are not ends: they are marks of growth and means to its continuing."[6] In short, education, properly understood, is not a preparation for life; it *is* life.

In school or out, most of us never begin to think reflectively until we are faced with some problem it is in our personal interest to solve. (This is why Deweyan education emphasizes individualism.) But our slowness to think reflectively does not mean we are lazy; it means, rather, that we are creatures of routine, or habit. Habit is akin to the automatic pilot that flies the airplane when the pilot is not in manual control. If we had to think about everything we did in life, the results would be debilitating. Habit does the work of thinking for us; it carries us along, as it were, to our destinations.

But what happens when the old, accepted ways of doing things are impeded? Whatever sets us to doubting what we had taken for granted stimulates reflective thinking. All reflective thinking, for Dewey, is born in problem and doubt.

Dewey's analogy of the forked road in *How We Think* (1910), written as a guide to teachers, contains the main features of what he means when he speaks of the operation of reflective thinking.

> A man traveling in an unfamiliar region comes to a branching of the road. Having no sure knowledge to fall back upon, he is brought to a standstill of hesitation and suspense. Which road is right? And how shall his perplexity be resolved? There are but two alternatives: he must either blindly and arbitrarily take his course, trusting to luck for the outcome, or he must discover grounds for the conclusion that a given road is right. Any attempt to decide the matter by thinking will involve inquiring into other facts, whether brought to mind by memory, or by further observation, or by both. The perplexed wayfarer must carefully scrutinize what is before him and he must cudgel his memory. He looks for evidence that will support belief in favor of either of the roads—for evidence that will weight down one suggestion. He may climb a tree; he may go first in this direction, then in that, looking, in either case, for signs, clues, indications. He wants something in the nature of a signboard or a map, and *his reflection is aimed at the discovery of facts that will serve this purpose.*[7]

This "perplexed wayfarer" is a person with an unsolved problem: how to get home. But Dewey applies this analogy to all human problems and to all humans. Only humans can ask the question and solve the riddle of how to get home. All other

**149**

creatures must rely on instinct to guide them. Humans are never entirely *lost* providing they know *how* to think about problems.

There are, of course, all kinds of problems in life, ranging from the trivial to the complex, but Dewey stresses that we are most assured of success in dealing with any problem if we take a step-by-step approach. This approach requires that we concentrate on immediate means rather than ultimate ends. There are no fixed goals or ends in human life, Dewey maintains, only specific ends-in-view; when they are achieved, they become means to other ends-in-view. He illustrates this idea by suggesting that the hard-drinker who wants to reform will succeed only if he stops drinking now and finds something else to take the place of the habitual dependence on alcohol. Good intentions and wishful thinking will get this man nowhere.

We make progress toward the solution of any problem only by committing ourselves with absolute seriousness to the first step. "The first or earliest means," says Dewey, "is the most important *end* to discover."[8] Without the discovery of that first means, which is also an end, no further progress is possible. Like laying stepping stones across a stream, the first stone we lay is the most important, for it becomes the platform from which we will lay the second stone, the third stone, and so on, stone by stone, until we have crossed the stream.

Dewey conceives of life as presenting ever new and unexpected problems. But for him this feature of life is not a source of despair. He sees it, rather, as an opportunity for reflective individuals to steadily grow. Dewey is a philosopher who is exhilarated by the discovery of the essentially temporal character of the Darwinian world. Only in an unfinished world is human improvement possible; only where all is genuinely unfinished can something yet be done. In so insisting, Dewey takes a pioneering, exploratory stance toward the future. For him, change means the excitement of novelty. Time still remains to think and do and accomplish, to make a difference in ourselves and to make over a civilization.

This stance toward the future explains in large part why the concept of education is central to Dewey's philosophy. With the young, one can begin anew—if only one can free education itself from the habits and prejudices that have made it the weapon of the vested interests and encrusted traditions of any given society. Dewey's ideas about thinking and education embody a reformer's zeal. The day is ours, he declares. Let us improve it with thinking as our instrument and education as our means. The possibilities of improvement are boundless providing we know how to think reflectively.

# Dewey on
# What Ought I to Do?

No area of human life, in Dewey's opinion, presents a greater challenge to reflective thinking than morality. Our discussion of Dewey's theory of morality is based on Part II of *Ethics* (1908), a textbook that he wrote in collaboration with James H. Tufts, and *Human Nature and Conduct* (1922).

Dewey recognizes *impulse, habit,* and *intelligence*[9] as the three distinctive components of human nature (just as Plato recognizes *appetite, spirit,* and *reason,* or Freud *id, ego,* and *superego*). By *impulse* Dewey means the psychological dispositions (e.g., fear, aggression) and physical needs (e.g., food, shelter, sex) we are born with. By *habit* he means usual modes of activity and behavior into which impulse is channelled (war, farming, building houses, marriage). By *intelligence* he means the reflective thinking by which we modify habit.

Impulses are unlearned and, as such, are unchanging in human nature. "I do not think it can be shown," Dewey says, "that the innate needs of men have changed since man became man or that there is any evidence that they will change as long as man is on the earth."[10] Habits, on the other hand, are acquired or learned and, as such, are subject to change. Everybody has to eat, but not everybody has to eat the same foods or follow the same rules of etiquette for eating. Foods and rules of etiquette differ from place to place. Because we have learned our habits initially, we have the capacity to modify current ones and learn new ones if we have sufficient cause for doing so.

No habits are more ingrained than moral habits. In order to bring about changes in morality, the most conscientious thinking and effort are required. Most of us, Dewey supposes, never think about morality because we don't have to. Impulse is channelled into "customary morality,"[11] which provides the rules and standards of conduct and prescribes the proper ends of life. So long as the customary morality of the social group to which we belong (the clan, the family, the church, the nation) is firmly in place, and we as individuals adhere to this morality, we don't think about it. We know what to do and what not to do according to the rules and standards of our social group(s). All that customary morality requires of us is obedience.

But what happens when customary morality fails to give the required guidance? "This failure happens," says Dewey, "when old institutions break down; when invasions from without and inventions and innovations from within radically alter the course of life."[12] With the failure of customary morality, "Thinking has to operate creatively to form new ends."[13] It must reestablish the required guidance on how to live and what to live for. Thus, Dewey posits two kinds of morality: "customary" and "reflective."[14] The first is uncritical and habit bound; the second is critical and creative.

Reflective morality gives no blind allegiance to any socially held standards or rules; it depends upon context. The biblical rule "Thou shalt not kill" would not have originated in the warring society Homer depicts in the *Iliad*, where killing is an accepted way of life; it is a matter of honor and survival. No rule or standard is absolute; each must be understood as it relates to particular times, places, and peoples.

Just as reflective morality does not blindly submit to any socially held rules or standards, so, too, it does not reject rules or standards simply because they belong to the past or to societies different from one's own. Dewey recognizes that even attitudes and positions far removed from us in time may be used toward satisfactorily resolving present moral questions of right or wrong, good or bad, better or worse. Reflective thinking may yield results now that are connected with the social wisdom of the past. Old answers may still be good ones or, possibly, the only ones of their kind. Any answer is worthy of respect only insofar as it practically responds to a present question. Rules and standards of the past afford legitimate materials for our use, but they are to be viewed critically and applied "instrumentally."

Dewey maintains that the basic issue in reflective morality is one of evaluating the nature and quality of the life we want to lead. "The question of what ends a man should live for," he says, "does not arise as a general problem in customary morality."[15] It arises, however, as the paramount question in reflective morality, wherein no ready-made end-in-view is presented. Indeed, from the standpoint of reflective morality, we cannot assume there is any one authentic end-in-view. When we look about us and consider the way life is actually lived, we discover that human beings are interested in a great variety of goods, which they pursue individually as their ends-in-view. Reflective morality, by introducing a personal dimension into the problem of the conduct of life, renders the question of goals in life inseparable from the question of my goals in life.

Ends, or goals, shape and form character, or the self. They give substance and meaning to the kind of person we are and therefore should be carefully considered. But the consideration of goals poses a major problem. If goals do not present themselves as ready-made, then how can we know what goals to seek? Does Dewey not set us out upon a journey without a map? Not quite! On the subject of goals he offers shrewd counsel:

> Except as the outcome of arrested development, there is no such thing as a fixed, ready-made, finished self. Every living self causes acts and is itself caused in return by what it does. All voluntary action is a remaking of self, since it creates new desires, instigates to new modes of endeavor, brings to light new conditions which institute new ends. Our personal identify is found in the thread of continuous development which binds together these changes. In the strictest sense, it is impossible for the self to stand still; it is becoming, and becoming for the better or the worse. It is in the *quality* of becoming that virtue resides. We set up this and that end to be reached, but *the* end is growth itself. Many a person gets morally discouraged because he has not attained the object upon which he set his resolution, but in fact his moral status is determined by his movement in that direction, not by his possession. If such a person would set his thought and desire upon the *process* of evolution instead of upon some ulterior goal, he would find a new freedom and happiness. It is the next step which lies within our power.[16]

Here Dewey suggests that it's appropriate to try an indirect approach in thinking about goals. Admittedly, we may have some remote goal in view, such as becoming a professional athlete or a renowned scientist. But the prudent approach is to think of the immediate next step, not of the remote end. Looking at the remote end may lead to discouragement and paralysis. In thinking about goals, the main thing is to concentrate on the means, or as Dewey says, "the process of evolution."

In fact, from Dewey's viewpoint the means indicate the legitimacy of our goals. If we are not fascinated with language, the goal of becoming a poet is inappropriate; if we are not given to hard study, the goal of becoming a medical doctor is untenable; if we do not like to practice, the goal of becoming a concert pianist is impractical. Dewey's general view of human conduct does not countenance any such vague question as What is the meaning of life? The meaning of life is always in the making. If there is any certainty about goals in life, it's more a matter of hindsight than foresight. We may ultimately look back from some pinnacle of achievement, but only because we kept our eye on the immediate sequential tasks in the process of reaching that goal. If we are not interested in the means, the goals themselves are illusory.

In response to the question What ought I to do? Dewey does not offer a categorical answer. His theory of morality, along with the rest of his philosophy, is based on the insight the human beings never arrive at a state of completion; they are always in that process of becoming. If there is a general rule for conducting one's life, it's to become all that we are capable of becoming.

## Dewey on for What Can I Hope?

Dewey does not adhere to any traditional concept of God. He wrote a short book on the subject of religion, *A Common Faith,* in which he suggests that the idea of a personal Creator who oversees his creation is purely a throwback to an age of myth. From his outlook, there are no eternal verities, only proximate, relative "goods," which are achieved in the course of living. When any good—or that which enhances the quality and enjoyment of life—has been achieved, nothing permanent has been realized. The very success of the achievement of goods creates the need for new goods and new efforts to reach them. The life of the individual and the life of humanity are in a process of constant change. No good is fixed; it's only a means to a further one.

From Dewey's perspective, personal freedom of choice makes the pursuit of goods possible. This freedom, which is called *free will* in traditional terminology, is the capacity of reflective men and women to make real decisions in situations where significant alternatives exist.

By no means is all human functioning the result of un-bounded free choice. Human freedom always operates within certain definite limits. The human animal has a specific physical structure that can function and survive only if a number of en-vironmental conditions prevail. We must have air to breathe, water to drink, and conform to natural laws, like that of gravity. Furthermore, our freedom is always limited by our personal habits, as well as by the customs that are laid down by the social groups to which we belong. To the extent that human life is limited, we may say it is determined; to the extent that we can make choices within limits, we may say it is free. Life may be aptly compared to a game of tennis. There are stated, established rules (representing determinism) that every player is required to follow. Yet, within that broad framework, innovation (representing freedom of choice) is possible.

One of Dewey's major contributions to the concept of freedom, however, is the insight that freedom of choice can actual-ly alter our limits. Centuries ago the game of tennis was played predominantly by royalty, for entertainment, on grass courts, with crude equipment. Today, the game of tennis is primarily played by professionals, on artificial courts, with sophisticated equipment. What has brought about the changes in tennis if not that in-dividuals made choices about how the game can and should be played?

Freedom of choice is inextricably bound up with the capacity of human beings to think and to stand aside temporari-ly from the flux of an immediate situation. During a typical moment of reflection, we imaginatively examine and rehearse the different possibilities, options, or goods that are open to us, finally choosing the one we wish to see actualized. The pluralis-tic potentialities in nature and human life confront us with occasions for making choices that count from among alterna-tives that are real.

If there is any candidate for a general concept of good in Dewey's philosophy—a good that he sees as the legitimate object of hope for every human being—it would be *growth*. His deep concern for the growth of the individual is clearly expressed in his declaration on the true purpose of government, business, religion, art, and education.

> That purpose is to set free and to develop the capacities of human individuals without respect to race, sex, class or economic status. And this is all one with saying that the test of their value is the extent to which they educate every individual into the full stature of his possibility.[17]

This declaration shows Dewey's own ruling commitment to the goals of an open democratic society. His concern for developing the capacities of the individual goes hand in hand with his conviction that democracy—to the extent that it encourages freedom of choice and creative activity on the part of the individual—is the wisest political instrument yet known for developing those capacities and enriching the possibilities of everyone. His vision of an open democratic society is one in which free interplay and cooperation among individuals results in mutual growth. We are, necessarily, social beings. What we can hope for and work toward, Dewey urges, is a society where contact with the lives of others challenges, varies, and fructifies the life of each individual.

## Implications of the Deweyan Image of Human Nature

Dewey's image of the human being as a thinker and a doer who is immersed in change resonates with us. It lies near the surface of modern life, especially life within American society. It's unlikely that Dewey's theory of education, which is a manifestation of his image of human nature, would have gained so solid a foothold in American schools if it had not appealed to sentiments and values that were already deeply seated in the consciousness of the American people. Precisely because we embrace this image, we lack objectivity in trying to describe it. We are like people in the dark trying to describe an elephant according to the particular part of the elephant we happen to touch. Nonetheless, let's try to attain some objectivity on this image by spelling out four of its major contentions. Keep in mind that these are Dewey's contentions as he puts his philosophical stamp on an evolutionary theory of human nature.

The *first contention* is that the human being is what he or she is, not what he or she was. No period or hour of history has greater authority than the present period and hour. The stage at which humanity has arrived is more authentic than any which may be selected from preceding periods.

If by some means we could step back in time and mix with people of a distant age, we would have good cause to doubt either their view of life or ours. Trees, mountains, and skies would look the same, but they would not be seen by those around us as we would see them. In all likelihood, their view of these natural phenomena would embrace a mythical and religious significance that was lacking for us.

We would know what common sense is and what constitutes normal behavior, but so would the people among whom we found ourselves. Their understanding of common sense and normal behavior, however, would probably differ from our own. We would question much of what they took for granted and be amazed that they were so unquestioning in their assumptions. They, on the other hand, would call into question much of what we would take for granted.

The *second contention* is that we are conditioned and shaped by the particular period and environment to which we belong. Consciously or unconsciously, we are to some extent held captive by modes of thought and feeling not of our own making. We inherit them by virtue of being born to a particular people, in a particular time and place. It's not easy to break free—some see no reason to do so—but it's not impossible. Among all living creatures, the human being alone is capable of some degree of detachment from his or her temporal matrix.

This emphasis on the possibility of detachment constitutes the *third contention* of the Deweyan image. Though influenced by evolutionary thought, this image rejects any rigid doctrine of biological evolution. Darwin and the early evolutionists thought of the environment as a relatively stable set of conditions to which organisms had to be adapted lest they perish. Dewey, on the other hand, sees that from remote antiquity, humans have refused to passively accept the environment in which they happen to dwell. From the beginning of history, humans have been trying to cajole or compel the forces of nature about them. In the past, their methods have been basic: simple weapons for hunting and fighting, simple devices for catching fish, simple implements for tilling the ground. Albeit basic, those methods show the human bent, *intention* to have a hand in our own destiny. All but at the mercy of nature, human beings have nevertheless found it possible to either detach themselves from nature or extend the area in which they are able to attain their ends.

The *fourth contention* of the Deweyan image is that, after revising the environment to fit ourselves, we then go on to fit ourselves to the revised environment. The human process of changing the world makes us, in a true sense, creators of our own nature. Whenever we confront a situation that is problematic, we begin to think and ask questions. The first question we are likely to ask is What is wrong with the situation? The second question we are likely to ask is How can I correct the situation? If we discover we have too little food to carry us through the winter, we may reflect that next season we must plant more, earlier and be more diligent in our methods of cultivation. In the course of centuries, such problematic situations and the solutions people have arrived at to correct them have perceptibly altered the kind of creatures we are.

Other able thinkers deny that humans have any hand in shaping their own nature. They argue that human nature is the same as it's always been; only the garments of culture in which it's draped have changed over the centuries. But Dewey sees the invention of technological means and the subduing of natural forces for human ends changing the essential nature of the creature who is inventing and subduing. Human nature is reflected in its artifacts; it is also extended by them. With the invention of the atomic bomb and the spaceship, we are now what we never were, and what we are is not what we will be. Human nature is not fixed, but malleable; humanity's future is not determined, but open-ended. To adhere to the Deweyan image is to feel oneself unencumbered by the past, self-reliant in the present, and optimistic about the future.

# Suggestions for Discussion and Study

1.  Dewey does not offer a formal theory of evil, but he infers that evil is not the product of some permanent instinct or impulse in human nature that cannot be altered. It is, rather, the product of the special ways a society has shaped and conditioned human impulses. Christianity has taught that sin, or evil, represents some inveterate flaw in human nature. Dewey holds that evil is learned. Which of these views do you find most credible? Why?

2.  Harvey Cox is a contemporary religious thinker who characterizes the pragmatic person in the following manner:

    He approaches problems by isolating them from irrelevant considerations, by bringing to bear the knowledge of different specialists, and by getting ready to grapple with a new series of problems when these have been provisionally solved. Life for him is a set of problems, not an unfathomable mystery. He brackets off the things that cannot be dealt with and deals with those that can. He wastes little time thinking about "ultimate" or "religious" questions. And he can live with highly provisional solutions (*The Secular City: Secularization and Urbanization in Theological Perspective* [New York: The Macmillan Co., 1966], p. 63).

    One of the basic traits of modern society, Cox suggests, is the willingness on the part of many persons to deal with their immediate problems in favor of any questions concerning the ultimate end, or the ultimate purpose of life. This is the pragmatic attitude. Is it a healthy attitude? Why or why not?

3.  It might be argued that for Dewey the human being does not have a nature. The human being is a creature who makes choices, takes risks, makes mistakes, retreats, reorganizes his or her action, and persists. In and through the interplay with environment, the human being constantly changes. Rather than saying the human being has a nature, perhaps it's more appropriate to say that the human being pursues a nature that he or she never completely possesses. Robert Jay Lifton, in an essay titled "Protean Man" (*Partisan Review*, Vol. XXXV, No. 1 [Winter 1968], pp. 13–27), suggests that a dominant theme of

**159**

modern culture is the pursuit of one's own nature. Lifton sees this theme exemplified in such contemporary works of literature as Saul Bellow's *The Adventures of Augie March,* Jack Kerouac's *On the Road,* J. P. Donleavy's *The Ginger Man,* and Günter Grass' *The Tin Drum.* Undertake a study of one or more of these works in light of the Deweyan image of human nature. Notice how the author you study *evaluates* the notion that we pursue our own nature. Does the author find this notion appealing or threatening? Do you find it appealing or threatening?

4. Dewey does not claim that all habits are wrong or bad for a person. Without habits, we would lack essential direction in the moment. Take the following as a working definition of habit: *a habit is an inclination acquired by repetition, activated and expressed with little or no thought, and performed without much resistance.* What are your good and bad habits? What are the good and bad habits of certain persons with whom you are acquainted?

5. In saying a habit is good or bad, you are expressing a judgment, or a value. What values do you rely on in saying a habit is good or bad? (Dewey devotes an incisive sixty-seven-page monograph to the subject of valuation, titled *Theory of Valuation* [1939].)

6. Dewey recognizes two kinds of heredities: biological and cultural. We can do very little about biological heredity; biologically, we are what we are. We can do a good deal, Dewey implies, about cultural heredity; here we have a strong measure of freedom. Does Dewey underestimate the power of cultural heredity? To what extent are we bound by religion, politics, and economics?

7. You may find yourself pausing to consider implications of Dewey's theory of morality, as have many of his critics. For instance, Dewey suggests that any and all human convictions concerning what is right or wrong, good or bad, satisfactory or unsatisfactory are variable and arbitrary. There is no good, only a plurality of goods. Words like subjectivism and relativism attend discussions of Dewey's theory of morality. Yet, he does support a general notion of a good as something that contributes to the growth of a person, something that bears practical and propitious consequences in a person's life. Dewey's moral theory would make a lively subject for discus-

sion or for the writing of an essay. Is it possible, for instance, that some goods bear practical and propitious consequences in the lives of everyone?

# Further Reading

Dykhuizen, George. *The Life and Mind of John Dewey*. Carbondale: Southern Illinois University, 1978. A detailed biography with numerous photographs.

Geiger, George R. *John Dewey in Perspective*. New York: Oxford University Press, 1958. A non-technical interpretation.

Hook, Sidney. *John Dewey: An Intellectual Portrait*. New York: The John Day Co., 1939. A sympathetic treatment of Dewey as "the philosopher of American democracy."

Nathanson, Jerome. *John Dewey: The Reconstruction of the Democratic Life*. New York: Frederick Ungar Publishing Co., 1967. Stresses the evolutionary aspect of Dewey's thought.

Scheffler, Israel. *Four Pragmatists: A Critical Introduction to Peirce, James, Mead, and Dewey*. London: Routledge & Kegan Paul, 1974. Explores the interdisciplinary implications of Dewey's thought and that of three other major pragmatists.

# Notes

1. Friedrich Nietzsche, *Thus Spake Zarathustra*, trans. Thomas Common, in *The Philosophy of Nietzsche* (New York: The Modern Library, 1954), p. 125.
2. Nietzsche, *Beyond Good and Evil*, trans. Helen Zimmern, in *The Philosophy of Nietzsche*, op. cit., pp. 429–430.
3. Nietzsche, *Thus Spake Zarathustra*, op. cit., p. 10.
4. Nietzsche, *The Geneology of Morals*, trans. Horace B. Samuel, in *The Philosophy of Nietzsche*, op. cit., p. 653.
5. John Dewey, *The School and Society*, rev. ed. (Chicago: The University of Chicago Press, 1929), pp. 135–136.
6. John Dewey, *Reconstruction in Philosophy*, enlarged ed. (Boston: The Beacon Press, 1965), p. 185.
7. Jo Ann Boydston, ed., *How We Think: A Restatement of the Relation of Reflective Thinking to the Educative Process*, by John Dewey, vol. 8 of *John Dewey: The Later Works, 1925–1953* (Carbondale: Southern Illinois University Press, 1986), pp. 121–122.

8. John Dewey, *Human Nature and Conduct: An Introduction to Social Psychology* (New York: The Modern Library, 1957), p. 35.
9. Ibid., pp. 172–180.
10. Jo Ann Boydston, ed., "Does Human Nature Change?" by John Dewey, vol. 13 of *John Dewey: The Later Works, 1925–1953* (Carbondale: Southern Illinois University Press, 1988), p. 286.
11. Jo Ann Boydston, ed., *Ethics*, by John Dewey and James H. Tufts, vol. 7 of *John Dewey: The Later Works, 1925–1953* (Carbondale: Southern Illinois University Press, 1985), p. 184.
12. Ibid., pp. 184–185.
13. Ibid., p. 185.
14. Ibid., p. 162.
15. Ibid., p. 184.
16. Ibid., p. 306.
17. John Dewey, *Reconstruction in Philosophy*, p. 186.

# CONCLUSION

Let's briefly summarize the ground we have covered in this book before carrying our reflections further. The subject of human nature, we have said, deals with the question of the difference between human beings and all other creatures. We have indicated that images of human nature are instruments of thought that enable us to orient ourselves to life. And we have divided images into two basic kinds: partial and complete. Complete images respond to Kant's three basic questions of existence: What can I know? What ought I to do? For what can I hope? Partial images may respond to one or two of these questions, but they do not respond to all of them.

Each of the six thinkers we have studied presents a complete image of human nature. Confucius presents an image of the human being as essentially a social creature; Sophocles, as a creature of courage; Augustine, as a creature of faith; Hobbes, as an egoistic creature; Hume, as a creature of sympathy; and Dewey, as a creature of change.

To compare and contrast these images one with the other is to see basic areas of similarity and difference. On the question What can I know? Confucius, Sophocles, and Augustine agree that the power of human intellect is linked to and inspired by the power of the gods or God. Hobbes, Hume, and Dewey see the human intellect as an autonomous power.

On the question What ought I to do? Confucius, Sophocles, and Augustine recognize a moral principle in the universe that enjoins humanity to a universal norm of conduct. For Confucius, this principle is the Way; for Sophocles, it is justice; for Augustine, it is providence. This concept of a moral principle in the universe has little or no place in the thought of Hobbes, Hume, and Dewey. For them, humanity is on its own, working out its own norms of conduct in the temporal process of history.

On the question For what can I hope? only Augustine believes clearly in life beyond the grave. Confucius chooses to remain silent on the subject; Sophocles does not harbor the prospect of life beyond the grave; Hobbes undermines the Augustinian-Christian belief; Hume spurns it; and Dewey seems wholly preoccupied with the things of this life.

A distinct pattern emerges among these images as we move from the ancient thought of Confucius, Sophocles, and Augustine to the modern thought of Hobbes, Hume, and Dewey. With the latter three thinkers, we notice an increasing tendency to talk about human nature without reference to concepts of the divine. It would be wrong to assume, however, that the ancient images that embrace concepts of the divine are simply things of the past. They have a way of existing alongside of and commingling with modern secular images and for exhibiting their strength in the very vehemence with which secular thinkers resist them.

The six images we have studied span twenty-five hundred years of human culture, but how much time is that in relation to the life of the universe? The astronomer and astrophysicist Robert Jastrow writes:

> Calculations based on the present positions of galaxies show that [the original explosion of the universe] occurred twenty billion years ago. . . . This is a very long time. The sun and the earth have only existed for four and a half billion years, and life has been on the earth for even less time than that. Humanity has existed on our planet for only one million years, which is less than one ten-thousandth as long as the age of the Universe.[1]

These gigantic intervals of time begin to place human existence in a cosmic perspective. The twenty-five hundred years spanned by our images are barely a tick on the cosmic clock.

Of these one million years humanity has existed, only about seven thousand belong to what we call *history*. What we know of humanity before those years we owe largely to archaeology and paleontology. The oldest known fossil remains of the truly modern human, *Homo sapiens*, are about forty thousand years old. Beyond those forty thousand years lie oceans of time that challenge the imagination. The more we reflect, the more it becomes obvious that these six images could not possibly embrace all of the ways human beings have understood their own nature in the course of human life on the planet.

But they are nevertheless extremely important, because they represent ways of understanding human nature that are available to us. Whether or not you or I as individuals claim any one of these six images as our own, each one is claimed by many persons in the world today as being the image of human nature. These six images are living: they have given orientation to human lives in the past, give orientation in the present, and will continue to do so in the future. It matters little that these six images do not embrace all of the ways human beings have understood their own nature in the course of human life on the planet. It is enough to say of them—as well as of other living images we have not studied in this book—that they enable us to orient ourselves to life now.

A common theme runs throughout myth, theology, philosophy, and science concerning humanity's origin and destiny. Whatever frame of reference is used, it's understood that humanity had a beginning and will also have an end. Whether humanity is closer to its beginning than its ending is a question of profound interest, especially since we now have in our hands the technological means to be the agents of our own annihilation. But when and how the ending will come is not necessarily the most important question.

The most important question is What will we do with our life while we are here? Between our personal beginning and ending, our birth and death, we have the opportunity to take responsibility for our own actions and aims, to formulate and live out an image of human nature that we are willing to pass on to our children and grandchildren. It's one thing to live and quite another to live *deliberately*. The study of complete images of human nature is an intrinsic part of educating ourselves, sorting out what is truly worth living for.

We have consciously set our course in this book to avoid the deeply philosophical question of whether an image is true, whether it matches up with some reality in the world outside it. Not only would that question lead into the roiling waters of metaphysics, where we are not prepared to sail, it would also be contrary to our objectives. We have tried to suggest that what people believe about human nature has the semblance of truth, and this semblance of truth in the lives of individuals takes on the significance of the real thing.

Inherent to our approach, of course, is the philosophical assumption that we never penetrate human nature as a *ding an sich* ("thing-in-itself"). This assumption might be vigorously disputed, but it nevertheless belongs to the character of this book. Our hope is that in having seen images of human nature presented somewhere, readers may begin to see them exhibited everywhere—in novels, plays, movies—and thus begin to assess the importance of images of human nature as they pertain to our lives.

# Note

1. Robert Jastrow, *The Enchanted Loom: Mind in the Universe* (New York: Simon & Schuster, A Touchstone Book, 1981), p. 16.

# INDEX

Academics, 72
Adeodatus, 71
Aeschylus, 46, 47
Alaric (k. of the Visigoths), 83
Alembert, Jean D', 123
Alexander the Great, 69
Ambrose (bishop of Milan), 72, 73
American Revolution, 120
*Analects*, 26
Ancestor worship, 23
Ancient Greece (*see* Greece (ancient))
Annihilation
    Augustine and, 85
    Darwinian theory and, 10
Anthropology, 6–7
Anti-intellectualism, 131
Aquinas, Thomas, 95
Arendt, Hannah, 85
Aristophanes, 46
Aristotle, 8
    Augustine and, 71
    Dewey compared, 148
    Islamic culture and, 95
    scholasticism and, 95
Arnold, Matthew, 61
Arts of peace (Wen), 33–34 (*see also* Peace; War)
Assumption
    defined, 12
    human nature and, 12–15
Athens, 48
Aubrey, John, 99
Augustine, Saint, 7, 14, 16, 69–92

biography of, 70–74
cultural background of, 69–70
Dewey compared, 148
evil and, 78–79
human nature and, 86–89
love and, 80–82
scholasticism and, 96
What Can I Hope question, 82–86
What Can I Know question, 74–78
What Ought I to Do question, 78–82
will and, 79–80
Augustus Caesar, 69
Authority, 108–109, 110
Autonomous human nature, 3 (*see also* Human nature)
Axial period, 45

Bacon, Francis, 98
Barth, Karl, 120
Becker, Carl, 119, 134
Benedict, Ruth, 13
Berkeley, George, 125
Bible
    Augustine and, 73, 76, 84, 86, 88
    Enlightenment and, 120
    Genesis, 45, 69, 84
    Hume and, 125
    Puritans and, 98
    *Vulgate*, 96
Boswell, James, 133
Buddha, 6, 45
Byzantine culture, 95, 96

Camus, Albert, 14, 61
Causation, 126, 127
Cavendish, William, 98, 99
Charles I (k. of England), 100
Charles II (k. of England), 98, 100
Child rearing, 4–5
China
    culture of, 23–24
    Dewey and, 145
Chipman, Harriet Alice, 146
Chou dynasty, 23, 27
Christianity, 14, 16
    Augustine and, 70, 73–74
    Darwin and, 143
    Hobbes and, 110
    humanism and, 96–97
    Hume and, 125, 130, 134–135
    imagery of, 6
    love and, 80–82
    Manicheanism and, 71
    politics and, 84–85
    Roman Empire and, 69, 83
    scholasticism and, 96
    Spain and, 95
Chronology (see Time)
Chun-tzu (noble-mindedness), 30–31
Cicero, 83
    Augustine and, 69, 71
    Hume and, 121, 128–129
Clinton, Sir Gervase, 99
Cochrane, Charles Norris, 82–83, 86
Common sense, 157
Competition, 106–107
Concentration camps (Nazi Germany),
    61–62
Confucius and Confucianism, 7, 16,
    23–24, 45
    biography of, 24–26
    cultural background of, 23–24
    human nature and, 36–38
    What Can I Hope question, 34–36
    What Can I Know question, 26–28
    What Ought I to Do question, 28–
    34
Conrad, Joseph, 61
Constantine (e. of Rome), 69
Copernicus, Nicolaus, 11, 97
Creel, H. G., 35
Cromwell, Oliver, 98, 100

Cultural human nature, 3 (see also Cul-
    ture; Human nature)
Culture
    Augustine and, 69–70, 71
    Confucius and, 23–24, 31
    Dewey and, 143–144
    Hobbes and, 95–97
    human nature and, 7
    Hume and, 119–120
    thought and, 12
    tragic heroism and, 45–48
Cynicism, 111–112
Cyrus (k. of Persia), 45

Dante Alighieri, 96
Darwin, Charles, 6, 8–12, 17, 144
    Dewey and, 158
    philosophy and, 143–144
Definition, 103–104
Deism, 34–35
Democracy
    Confucius and, 28
    Dewey and, 156
    Hobbes and, 99
Descartes, René, 99, 236
Detachment, 157–158
Determinism
    Darwin and, 11–12
    predestination and, 85
    tragic heroism and, 54, 57
    (see also Free will)
Dewey, John, 7, 8, 17, 143–162, 165–166
    biography of, 144–146
    cultural background of, 143–144
    human nature and, 156–159
    What Can I Hope question, 154–156
    What Can I Know question, 147–
    151
    What Ought I to Do question, 151–
    154
Diderot, Denis, 123
Dike (justice), 55–56 (see also Justice)
Dissent, 14
Donation of Constantine, 96

Education
    Confucius and, 28–29
    Dewey and, 148–149, 156–157
Egoism, 105–106, 108, 109

Elizabeth I (q. of England), 97
Empiricism, 125–126
England, 97–98, 100, 101
Enlightenment, 17
    described, 119
    Hume and, 123, 125–126, 131, 134
Environment (see Nature)
Epictetus, 61
Euclid, 99
Euripides, 46, 47
Evil
    Augustine and, 78–79, 80, 88
    Hobbes and, 105–106
Evolutionary theory, 8–9 (see also Darwin, Charles)
Existentialism, 61
Experience, 128

Faith, 76–77
Fan Ch'ih, 29
Faulkner, William, 61
Feudalism, 23
Five Classics of Confucianism, 24
Foot, Philippa, 129
Four Books of Confucianism, 24–25
France, 121, 123
Frankl, Victor E., 61–62
Free will
    Augustine and, 78, 79–80
    Darwin and, 11–12
    Dewey and, 155–156
    (see also Determinism)
French Revolution, 120
Freud, Sigmund, 151
Fromm, Eric, 37–38

Galileo Galilei, 97, 99
    Hobbes and, 101
    Newton and, 119
Genesis, 45, 69, 84 (see also Bible)
Germany, 61–62, 96
Gilson, Étienne, 76
Goals, 153–154
God
    Augustine and, 76–77, 79, 86, 88
    Christianity and, 6
    Darwin and, 143
    Dewey and, 154
    Hume and, 124–125, 134–135

Jesus and, 89
    modernity and, 166
    (see also Religion)
Good
    Augustine and, 74–76
    Confucius and (Jen), 29–30
    Hobbes and, 105–106
Goths, 83
Government (see Politics)
Grant, Roberta Lowitz, 146
Greece (ancient)
    axial period and, 45–46
    humanism and, 96

Habit, 151–152
Heaven, 35 (see also Immortality)
Hemingway, Ernest, 61
Hitler, Adolf, 112, 143
Hobbes, Thomas, 7, 16, 17, 95–115, 165–166
    biography of, 97–101
    cultural background of, 95–97
    Dewey compared, 148
    human nature and, 111–112
    Hume compared, 131
    What Can I Hope question, 110–111
    What Can I Know question, 101–105
    What Ought I to Do question, 105–109
Homer and Homeric tradition, 45–46
    Dewey and, 152
    Hobbes and, 101
    Sophocles and, 47, 54–55
Humanism
    culture and, 96–97
    Hume and, 124
Human nature
    assumptions in formulating, 12–15
    Augustine and, 70, 75, 79, 80, 86–89
    axial period and, 45
    child rearing and, 4–5
    culture and, 7 (see also Culture)
    Darwin and, 8–12, 143
    definitions of, 3
    Dewey and, 147–148, 149–150, 153, 156–159
    Hobbes and, 100, 109, 111–112

Hume and, 126, 130–132, 133, 134–135
imagery and, 4–7
Kant and, 6–7
Manicheanism and, 71–72
Neoplatonism and, 72–73
patterns of, 165–168
pragmatism and, 144
Sophocles and, 46–47, 49–50, 61–62
tragic heroism and, 54, 55, 58
types of, 3
Hume, David, 7, 17, 119–140, 165–166
biography of, 120–124
cultural background of, 119–120
human nature and, 134–135
What Can I Hope question, 132–134
What Can I Know question, 124–128
What Ought I to Do question, 128–132
Huxley, Thomas, 144

Ibsen, Henrick, 49
Image, 4–7
Imagination, 126
Immortality
Hume and, 133–135
tragic heroism and, 58–59
Incest, 52, 57
Individual and individualism
Dewey and, 149
Hobbes and, 106, 109, 111–112
Hume and, 133
social justice and, 36–38, 69–70
Instrumentalism, 144
Isaiah (prophet), 45, 76
Islam, 6, 95
Italy, 96

Jaeger, Werner, 47
James I (k. of England), 98
James, William, 144
Jaspers, Karl, 4, 45
Jastrow, Robert, 166
Jen (goodness), 29–30 (see also Good)
Jerome, Saint, 96
Jesus
Augustine and, 73, 76, 89
imagery and, 6

politics and, 84–85
Judaism, 6, 95
Julius Caesar, 69
Justice
Augustine and, 83
Hobbes and, 104
Plato and, 69–70
religion and, 70
tragic heroism and, 55–56

Kafka, Franz, 11
Kant, Immanuel, 5, 6–7, 15
Kepler, Johannes, 97
Kierkegaard, Sören, 6
Kitto, H. D. F., 55

Language, 103–104
Lao-Tzu, 45
Leibniz, Gottfried Wilhelm, 125
Lewis, C. W., 38
Li (propriety), 31–32
Locke, John, 125
Love
Augustine and, 80–92
social responsibility and, 83–84
Lovejoy, A. O., 4, 7
Loyalty, 37

Machiavelli, Niccolo di Bernardo, 100
Mahomet, 6 (see also Islam)
Mani, 71
Manicheanism, 71–72, 78–79
Marcel, Gabriel, 88
Marcus Aurelius, 61
Materialism, 102
Memory
Hobbes and, 103
Hume and, 126
Mersenne, Father, 99
Metaphysics, 101–102
Middle Ages, 95, 96
Milton, John, 145
Mirandola, Pico della, 97
Monica, 70, 73
Montaigne, Michel De, 61
Morality
Augustine and, 80–82
Confucius and (Te), 33
Dewey and, 151–154

Hobbes and, 104–105, 109
Hume and, 129–130, 131, 132
Nietzsche and, 143
Moses, 6
Muslims (see Islam)

Narcissism, 37–38
Natural selection, 9
Nature
    Darwin and, 143
    Dewey and, 147, 158
    Hobbes and, 106, 107
    Hume and, 126
Nazi Germany, 61–62
Neoplatonism, 72–73, 74–76, 78–79
Newton, Sir Isaac, 119, 143
Niebuhr, Reinhold, 14
Nietzsche, Friedrich, 143
Noblemindedness (Chun-tzu), 30–31

Oedipus legend, 16, 48–54
Olympian gods
    immortality and, 58–59
    Socrates and, 46
    Sophocles and, 47
    tragic heroism and, 55
Optimism, 119
Origin (Origenes Adamantius), 87
Original human nature, 3 (see also Human nature)

Patricide, 52, 57
Patricius, 70
Paul, Saint, 69, 70
Peace
    Augustine and, 88–89
    Confucius and (Wen), 33–34
    Hobbes and, 107, 111
    (see also War)
Pierce, Charles Sanders, 144
Perception
    Hobbes and, 107, 111
    Hume and, 126, 128
Persian Empire, 45
Philip of Macedon, 69
Physics, 101–102 (see also Science)
Plato, 86, 100, 151
    Augustine and, 69–70, 74–76, 79–80, 89

human nature and, 80
Hume and, 134, 135
scholasticism and, 95
Plotinus, 69, 72
Police state, 112
Politics
    Augustine and, 84–85
    Dewey and, 145
    Enlightenment and, 120
    Hobbes and, 108–109, 110, 111–112
    Hume and, 134
Pol Pot, 112
Pope of Rome, 96
Pragmatism, 144
Predestination, 85 (see also Determinism; Free will)
Propriety (Li), 31–32
Protestant Reformation (see Reformation)
Providence, 82
Puritans, 98, 100
Pythagoras, 45

Radical self-interest (see Egoism; Self-interest)
Ratiocination, 103
Rationality (see Reason)
Reason
    Augustine and, 75, 77
    axial period and, 45
    Hobbes and, 99, 102
    Hume and, 125–127
    Plato and, 70
    Socrates and, 46
    will and, 79–80
Reflective morality, 151–153 (see also Morality)
Reformation
    Augustine and, 87
    England and, 98
    humanism and, 96
Religion
    Augustine and, 69, 70, 73, 76
    Confucianism and, 32, 34–35
    Darwin and, 143
    Dewey and, 154–155
    England and, 98
    Enlightenment and, 119, 120

Greece (ancient) and, 46, 47 (*see also* Olympian gods)
Hobbes and, 100, 110
Hume and, 123, 124–125, 130, 132–133, 134–135
  image and, 6
  immortality and, 58–59
  justice and, 70
  Manicheanism and, 71–72
  modernity and, 166
  tragic heroism and, 55
  *See also entries under specific religions*
Renaissance
  humanism and, 96–97
  Hume and, 124
  science and, 119
Responsibility, 57
Roman Empire
  establishment of, 69
  fall of, 83, 88, 95
Romanianus, 71
Rousseau, Jean-Jacques, 123

Salvation, 82, 87
Sartre, Jean-Paul, 12
Scholasticism, 95–96
Science
  Hobbes and, 99, 101–102
  humanism and, 97
  Hume and, 124–125
  philosophy and, 143–144
  Renaissance and, 119
  time and, 166
Self-interest
  Hobbes and, 109, 111
  Hume and, 132
Seneca, 61
Sensation, 102–103
Shakespeare, William, 145
Shang dynasty, 23
Shang Ti, 23
Siddhartha Gautama, 6
Skepticism, 72
  Augustine and, 75
  Hume and, 128
Smith, Adam, 133
Social contract, 108–109
Socrates, 14, 46–47, 79
Sophocles, 7, 14, 16

biography of, 48
human nature and, 46–47, 61–62
Oedipus legend and, 48–54
tragic hero and, 47–48
What Can I Hope question, 58–60
What Can I Know question, 54–56
What Ought I to Do question, 56–58
(*see also* Tragic heroism)
Soul, 134–135
Spain, 95, 97–98
Spencer, Herbert, 144
Spinoza, Benedict, 125
Stalin, Josef, 112
State of nature (*see* Nature)
Suffering, 130
Supernatural, 28
Sympathy, 130–131, 134, 135 (*see also* Hume, David)

Tao, 27
Te (morality), 33 (*see also* Morality)
Technology
  Dewey and, 145
  Enlightenment and, 119–120
  (*see also* Science)
Thales, 45
Thinking, 148, 149 (*see also* Reason)
Thucydides, 99
Time
  Augustine and, 87
  modernity and, 166
Tradition, 27
Tragic heroism, 45–66
  conflicting views of, 14
  cultural background of, 45–48
  human nature and, 61–62
  Oedipus legend and, 48–54
  What Can I Hope question, 58–60
  What Can I Know question, 54–56
  What Ought I to Do question, 56–58
  (*see also* Sophocles)
Trojan War, 45
Truth, 74–76, 77
Tufts, James H., 151

Vaihinger, Hans, 5
Valerius (Bishop of Hippo), 73
Valle, Roman Lorenzo, 96
Vandals, 74

Vinci, Leonardo da, 97
Virgil, 121
Virtue (*see* Morality)
Voltaire, 120, 132
*Vulgate*, 96

Waley, Arthur, 26
Wallace, Alfred Russel, 8
War
    arts of peace and, 33–34
    Dewey and, 152

Hobbes and, 107, 111, 112
Hume and, 135
    (*see also* Peace)
*Wen* (arts of peace), 33–34 (*see also* Peace; War)
Westfall, Richard, 125
Willey, Basil, 132
Woolf, Virginia, 61

Yeats, William Butler, 27